JESUS ON PRAYER

ART NUERNBERG

EI
School of Biblical Training
FOLLOWING & PROCLAMING JESUS CHRIST AS LORD

Jesus on Prayer

Unless otherwise noted, scripture quotations taken from the New American Standard Bible® (NASB), Copyright © 1960, 1962, 1963, 1968, 1971, 1972, 1973, 1975, 1977, 1995 by The Lockman Foundation Used by permission. www.lockman.org

Printed in the United States of America

ISBN: 978-0-578-65890-2

Cover Photo: www.canva.com
Cover Design: Claire Borisuk

E.I. School of Biblical Training
700 N. Parker Rd.
Greenville, SC 29609, USA
www.eibibleschool.org

To Pam,
whose constant love and support
have been the Lord's great gift to me
as we have served Him together.

CONTENTS

INTRODUCTION

Why another book on prayer? An entire bookshelf in my study is devoted to works on prayer. These books were written over hundreds of years and represent almost every major theological outlook in Protestant Christianity. Esteemed theologians and Bible teachers are represented there, but they are joined by other somewhat obscure men who wrestled with the mystery of prayer and sought to lead their brothers and sisters into a richer experience of its potential. Considering the sheer number of volumes and the prestige of the people who wrote them, it does seem a bit arrogant to make another offering. So, why am I writing?

When I was a child, our family lived on two and a half acres in Western Pennsylvania. During those early years, I became fascinated with the game of golf. Finding a deserted bag of ancient clubs hanging in our garage, I grabbed one, stepped into our yard, and took my first swing. A group of not so proficient golfers saw me and offered a few general pointers. Armed with this information and an overly long club for my young body, I began to swing away.

Though we were certainly not in poverty, we did not have the extra money for me to play on a real course. But I was undaunted. I began designing a little course around our home. We also had no budget for broken windows, so I restricted my play to plastic practice balls. This was not a passing fancy. Over the next few years, I spent hours going around my little course, and as I grew into the clubs, I became quite good. However, the techniques for which I developed muscle memory in the backyard were far different than what was needed on an actual course with regulation golf balls.

Our family moved around for a couple years, disrupting my golf career. We finally settled in central Florida. At the age of fifteen, I got an after-school job retrieving balls at a driving range. The pay was bad, but the job came with perks. If the bins at the club house were full, I was free to hit all the shots I desired. And I did, taking thousands of swings whenever I had the opportunity. Although some balls went straight and long, many did not. My swing was so fundamentally flawed that consistency was impossible. About that time, I moved onto a course for the first time, where I played nearly every weekend. I always started with great hope and ended in anger. Inspired by pros on TV who made it look easy and duped by magazine articles that assured me that this or that change would solve my problems forever, I returned to repeat the cycle.

The problem was that my swing did not need a little tweaking; I needed to desert it and start over. But that would not be easy. Years of doing things the wrong way had fixed failure and frustration into my game. I never took the time to make the drastic move that was necessary. I still play golf occasionally for the sake of fellowship, but it is always a painfully embarrassing experience.

What does that have to do with a book on prayer? I have spent my adult life teaching at a discipleship training school where we instruct young people how to live the Christian life. Mastering the basics of prayer is a big part of that experience. Yet, students need more than a grasp of what is *said* about prayer; they need to *pray*. During the 1800s in his book, *Quiet Talks on Prayer,* S. D. Gordon expressed what remains true today:

> The great people of the earth today are the people who pray. I do not mean those who talk about prayer; nor those who say they believe in prayer;

nor yet those who can explain about prayer; but I mean these people who *take* time and *pray*.

Why do we *not* pray? It is certainly not because of a lack of need in our own lives or the lives of those around us. Nor is there a lack of encouragement on our Father's part. The most common reason people give for not praying is a lack of discipline. A consistent prayer life does demand a degree of discipline; however, I am not convinced that praying more is the answer. Playing more golf would not significantly improve my game. Using the wrong technique again and again does not improve the outcome.

My personal conviction is that failure in prayer is due to a lack of understanding of the basic principles of prayer. Too often, our praying is governed more by traditions than by a firm grasp of biblical teaching. Therefore, when the flesh and devil bring opposition to prayer, we have no solid base of faith. For many of my new students, prayer seems to have failed them. The only real benefit is that their conscience is soothed by the fact that they tried. They have little confidence, little expectation, that time with their Father has a vital impact on the world in which they live. Yet, unless Jesus Himself is lying, prayer does work.

Luke 11 records an event from late in the disciples' experience with the Lord. Jesus had committed followers who constantly lived in close fellowship with Him, and during those years Jesus taught them about prayer. On this occasion, Jesus had just returned from a time alone with His Father. Nothing about that was unique; the disciples had seen this before. But something was different on this occasion. An unnamed disciple, representing a larger group, approached Jesus. He had a simple request: "Lord, teach us to pray" (Luke 11:1). What prompted the question on that day? What caused this event to stick in the minds of the group and become part of the gospel story? To be honest, I do not know. The Bible does not say why they came, only that they asked. Let me venture some suggestions. I am simply speculating based on what I have learned about our difficulties in prayer.

Something of the significance of prayer had dawned on these men. In theory, we believe prayer is a vital part of a spiritual work. In practice, we are more impressed by the gifts and talents of people in leadership. Jesus was a dynamic leader, always intellectually ahead of His detractors and opponents; nobody ever trapped Him. He had the power and wisdom to deal with anything; nothing ever stumped Him. He was totally in control of Himself even under the most severe pressure; nothing ever threw Him off balance. The first suggestion is to note His greatness.

Still, I wonder if something else happened on that afternoon. I wonder if it was becoming clear that Jesus' public life was fueled by what happened in those long periods of private fellowship with His Father. The pressure was on from religious leaders. Perhaps the disciples realized that, if they were going to have strength to follow Him in the work, they would have to know what happened when He was praying.

Then there is a second matter. The disciples were Jews who had been to the synagogue all their lives. They had seen others pray and they themselves prayed. They knew what the Old Testament demonstrated and taught on prayer. They already had prayer lives; or, at least, we could say they had definite convictions about prayer. These convictions may have been their biggest hindrance to hearing the Lord when He spoke on the subject. But on this occasion, they were ready to be taught. They were ready for the Lord to retrain their "swing" in prayer.

When the disciples came to Jesus for instruction, He was more than willing to comply. I doubt there is a more thrilling moment for a teacher than when a student is ready to learn. On that day, these men were ready.

Years ago, before computers were commonplace, I determined to make a study of prayer in the New Testament. Taking an inexpensive copy of the Bible, I went from Matthew to Revelation looking for anything that was said about prayer, considering every prayer that was offered, and transcribing all the highlighted passages by hand. (I am deeply thankful for computers now.) If you made the same study, you would discover a difference in emphasis between Jesus in the Gospels and the apostles in the rest of the New Testament. Jesus teaches us how to pray; the apostles teach us how to use prayer.

This is a "how to" book. It concentrates on the principles Jesus taught about prayer. It covers everything He had to say on the subject. This book gives an exposition and application of Jesus' own words. My objectives are to help readers develop prayer habits with a solid biblical base, and to fortify their faith as they approach God daily.

This book is highly dependent for its form on a small volume by A. T. Pierson written in the 1800s, *Lessons in the School of Prayer*. In that work the author assembled all the teachings of Jesus on prayer, grouped them by subject, and arranged them as much as possible in chronological order. He detected ten progressive lessons concerning prayer. As I considered those passages many years ago, they became the framework for my own praying. I write to share what I have learned and what has become so valuable in my own experience. This book is dependent on Pierson's work in structure, but not so much in content. The author wrote for a late Victorian-era audience and addressed the conditions and mindsets of his age. We now find ourselves as Christians in a postmodern period. We need to consider what Jesus says in light of the challenges and pressures of the twenty-first century.

As we forge forward, let me also note that this is a textbook. Students at the Evangelical Institute really want to know how to walk with God. They do not receive a lofty degree or applause for their effort. I do not need to motivate them. I do not need to entertain them. This book is meant to give the students a tool to refresh them in their studies.

I make this book available to the church because I am convinced that there are struggling saints in local assemblies who know they are missing something in their prayer lives. They do not need to be motivated. The pressures of life have created ample motivation for them. They have heard the promises of God concerning prayer, and they know they fall short in experience. They are ready to join the frustrated disciples, ready to come to the Lord Himself to say, "Lord, teach us to pray."

Section One:

Privilege of Prayer

CHAPTER ONE

The Secret Place

When you pray, you are not to be like the hypocrites;
for they love to stand and pray in the synagogues and
on the street corners so that they may be seen by men.
Truly I say to you, they have their reward in full.
But you, when you pray, go into your inner room,
close your door and pray to your Father who is in
secret, and your Father who sees what is done in
secret will reward you.
Matthew 6:5-6

What is the essence of prayer? What is the fundamental benefit of praying? What happens in the unseen world when we pray? To put it in the form of a question which we often do not want to admit we ask, "Why should we pray anyway?" In His teaching, the Lord gives great promises concerning the potential of intercession. We can be tempted to jump straight to that subject as we think about prayer. But the Lord does not do that. Before He speaks of the potential of prayer, He addresses the essence of prayer. This is where He starts, and if we are going to be taught by Him, we cannot skip this lesson.

Jesus based His early ministry in the lakeside community of Capernaum. From there He launched His teaching and healing ministry. Miracles followed and His fame spread quickly around the region. Desperate people streamed to Jesus to experience His healing and His restoring work: lepers, epileptics, demoniacs, and paralytics. Through Him, divine power confronted the deepest physical and spiritual suffering of the day. People came hurting and bound; they departed healed and free. As the stories spread farther and His reputation grew, soon crowds from all over Galilee, and even from as far away as Jerusalem, flocked to experience the phenomena.

But more important than His healing ministry was His teaching. A dynamic quality permeated His thoughts. Empowered by the Spirit, He spoke with authority, answering the genuine needs of the hearts of His hearers. They sensed that Jesus knew their deepest pains, confusions, uncertainties, and concerns. And what is more, He had the cure. Little wonder that a group of men very quickly gathered around Him to follow Him as their master.

On the day Jesus preached the Sermon on the Mount, a very large crowd gathered (Matt. 5). Religious leaders are not mentioned in the account, but they were almost certainly there assessing this uncertified teacher. They would not have been alone in their concern. Whenever large groups of Jews gathered, the Roman overlords were wary. Jews had a habit of rebellion. Roman soldiers stationed in Capernaum were probably lurking on the outside, monitoring the situation.

However, those people were in the minority. The congregation that day was comprised primarily of common people who were just struggling to make sense of life. The need for healing, either for themselves or for loved ones, probably drew many. Others assembled specifically to hear Him teach. From the perspective of the Roman rulers or the religious elite from Jerusalem, the listeners were insignificant people. Indeed, in a generation or two, most of them would be completely forgotten. On that day, however, they had the attention of the Lord Himself.

Jesus ascended one of the high hills of Galilee, away from the noise of the towns, and sat down to teach. The subject of His carefully constructed message was a right relationship with God. The Master fully understood the people who listened to Him. He understood their frustrations, misunderstandings, disappointments, fears, hopes, and particularly their confusion about God. Confronting that confusion, He unveiled to them the potential of knowing God as their Father, and He called them to faith. In this message, we have the Lord's earliest recorded instructions on prayer.

The sermon contains both positive and negative elements. That bothers some. Why not focus on the positive? It sounds so pleasant, but real change demands more. All the people who sat on that hillside listening to Jesus had beliefs about life. Their minds were not blank sheets on which truth could be written. They had strongly-held opinions about every subject the Lord addressed, opinions which determined the course of their lives. Entering into the blessing Jesus offered was a two-step process. First, wrong thinking needed to be acknowledged and rejected. Second, the Lord's words had to be embraced and established in their hearts.

We need to face this in our own experience. Much of our difficulty in the Christian community arises from receiving the teaching of the Lord without also rejecting conflicting ideas. Too often, dual systems of thought occupy the same mind. To use the biblical phrase, we become "doubleminded." Real, releasing change in our lives requires accepting what God says as truth. But it also requires honestly facing how we think and consciously rejecting anything that contradicts Him. At the end of the sermon, the Lord calls this "building your house on the rock" (Matt. 7:24). This is particularly important in prayer. The congregation on the mountainside that day needed to face their own misconceptions of prayer and, more importantly, of God, and let Jesus' words heal them and lead them to rich fellowship with the Father.

How does the teaching on prayer fit into the sermon? Jesus gives a general warning: "Beware of practicing your righteousness before men to be noticed by them; otherwise you have no reward with your Father who is in heaven" (Matt. 6:1). Notice some key elements of what He says. He starts with, "Beware." In modern America, we tend to ignore that word. And why not? Warnings are plastered everywhere. I bought a cordless drill recently. The instruction manual began with nine pages of warnings. One would think that the tool was among the most difficult and dangerous tools to operate. Most of the warnings were trivial, probably to protect the maker from frivolous lawsuits. Honestly, I did not read them. However, there was a real danger there. Buried somewhere in all that verbiage, there may have been something I really needed to know. Too many warnings deaden their effect.

The Bible is not like that. When the Word of God gives a warning about a subject, there are two things to note with certainty. First, it is an area of difficulty to which we are all prone. Second, if we do not heed the warning, there are serious consequences.

What is it that we are prone to do? "Beware of practicing your righteousness before men to be noticed by them" (Matt. 6:1). There are activities that we should be involved in because of our relationship to God. Jesus calls these "practicing righteousness." We do them to honor God. In a true relationship with God, we live and we act with the Eternal God as our audience. Our actions may benefit others, but we do them because of our love for Him.

A problem arises here. We cannot see God. We cannot observe or even sense His approval. In our strong desire for self-validation, a subtle shift takes place. We continue to convince ourselves that we are living for God, but the people around us become our audience. We become actors, living to impress those around us or at least avoid their censure. Note again, we are all prone to this behavior. Sometimes this is positive, such as giving because we know people will be impressed. Sometimes it is negative, such as trying to out-perform others to display our spirituality. Either way, people become our audience and our reputation becomes our reward.

The word "beware" also indicates that there are serious consequences to this behavior. What is the danger? "Otherwise you have no reward with your Father who is in heaven" (Matt. 6:1). We need to stop and listen carefully to what the Lord is saying. We do not just lose *some* of the reward. We have *no* reward; the action means nothing to God. Think of Jesus' application of this to giving (Matt. 6:1-4). When we give to the poor, if people are our audience and our reputation is our concern, their applause is the totality of our reward. It means nothing to God. Few of us believe that. Could a man give a billion dollars to the cause of the kingdom of God and not have any reward with God? Jesus says, "yes" if he has the wrong audience. This should scare us a little. It is much easier to live to impress people than to please God. We are all prone to hypocrisy, or play-acting. Nothing destroys a vital walk with God faster than hypocrisy. It robs us of our reward with God. Even worse, it triggers similar actions in others. Jesus told His disciples that this outlook destroyed the noble goals of the Pharisees. "Beware [there is that word again] of the leaven of the scribes and Pharisees which is hypocrisy" (Luke 12:1). When a little hypocrisy enters a group, it will quickly spread like yeast to become part of the whole. The Lord warns us to watch out for this.

Jesus' teaching on prayer in this sermon begins with an application of the principle from Matthew 6:1. Because of the danger described, He says,

When you pray, you are not to be like the hypocrites [actors]; for they love to stand and pray
in the synagogues and on the street corners so
that they may be seen by men. Truly I say to you,
they have their reward in full. But you, when you
pray, go into your inner room, close your door
and pray to your Father who is in secret, and your
Father who sees what is done in secret will reward you (Matt. 6:5-6).

To make His point, Jesus paints two extreme pictures.
The first extreme, which He calls hypocrisy, takes us first to
a religious gathering, then to a busy street (Matt. 6:5). Here
we are introduced to a person who loves to pray. He also
loves to be in the place where people gather to pray. He takes
the lead in the meeting, pouring out his praise and intercession before God. Yet, as he stands there in all his zeal, the
Lord calls him a hypocrite. Why? Because God is not his audience. He addresses God in the prayer, but the content is for
the congregation. He wants to be seen and admired as a man
of spirituality who knows the Scriptures and has mastered
the art of prayer. The people are his audience, watching his
performance. Their approval or lack of approval is his entire
reward. God does not care.

Jesus then gives further evidence of this man's commitment by observing him out on the street. There are many
who are bold in the congregation where supportive members hold the same convictions. When you take them into the
antagonistic everyday world, however, they cower and hide
their faith. Not this man. He loves to go to the busy street,
where everyone is carrying out life and business. There he
is a bold witness for God. He prays. To do that in Jesus' day
would require some powerful lungs, but he is undeterred.
Let others cringe; he will stand for God. Yet as he prays, the
crowd is his audience, not God. All his zeal means nothing

to God. Does that bother you? Does it not seem that there should be some benefit, some divine acknowledgement for such boldness? Jesus says, "No". There is no reward.

Jesus then presents a second extreme picture and encourages the listeners to paint themselves into it: "But you, when you pray" (Matt. 6:6). Those words must have been strange to the audience standing before Jesus. The religious leaders despised the common, spiritually uneducated masses. Like the rest of the human race, life's pain would force them to pray. Life forces almost everyone to pray at times. *But does the living God even care if I come?* That question must have been in many of their minds as Jesus taught. The Pharisees were worthy. They knew the Scriptures. They knew the words to use in prayer. They had the time to devote themselves to the service of God. What about the farmers, fishermen, tax collectors, and common workers gathered on that hill? Did God really listen to them? The Lord took a different tone altogether. He assumed that God was open to them and that they should take advantage of that fact. But when they did, they were also to completely avoid the outlook of the hypocrite.

"When you pray, go into your inner room" (Matt. 6:6). The homes of the people gathered to hear Jesus that day were very simple, generally only composed of one room. It was just a place for sleeping and storage. Most activity took place outside the home. In some homes, the inner room was a separate room, but generally it was more of a closet, or often just a cabinet. It was much like the broom closet we have in our home. If my wife was looking for me, she would not check that closet. If she opened it and found me there, she would be startled, to say the least. But that inner room is where the Master says to go, and this is His point: instead of going to a place where no one could miss you praying, go to the place where no one would find you, even if they were searching. When you get there, you are prepared to pray.

The very first principle of prayer is to get alone with God and address our words to Him. This is a pass/fail principle. If we miss here, nothing else matters. The prayer is worthless as far as God is concerned. When we get away from people and address our prayers to our Father, we personally have the attention of the Creator of the universe. He is indescribably great, powerful, and holy. And yet, at that moment, we have His complete attention. He is in secret. We cannot observe or necessarily detect Him, but He is there. Think again of the broom closet in our kitchen. Suppose I did get in it and was able to remain quiet. Suppose further that my wife came into the kitchen to make lunch. She would not be aware of my presence; I would be in secret. Secrecy does not change the reality of my presence.

This is important to know about prayer. I believe that God can communicate His presence to us. But a sense of God's presence is not necessary for prayer. The promise of Jesus in this verse is that the living God is present, even when we do not perceive Him. When we speak honestly to Him, He always takes notice.

If we succeed in getting alone with God, the promise which follows is this: "And your Father who sees what is done in secret will reward you" (Matt. 6:6). Note the careful wording the Lord uses. He does not say that when we get alone with our Father and pray to Him, He *hears* us. A survey of the Old Testament use of the word "hear" with regards to prayer reveals that it is always associated with a positive response to a request. But Jesus does not say this. We have a much more fundamental need than to "get answers" to prayer. We need to know God intimately. Prayer is not essentially a means of getting things from God. It is an opportunity to be with God, to have His attention, and to speak with Him from our hearts.

The exact meaning of the phrase translated, "sees what is done in secret," is difficult to determine. Jesus could be saying that the Father sees what is happening from His secret place. On the other hand, the emphasis could be on God seeing what no one else can see because we are praying in secret, hidden from view. The result is the same. Every secret communication of our hearts to the one who is our loving Father is noted by Him. Knowing that we have the attention of the eternal God should be enough to draw out prayer. But the Lord takes it a step further. Every honest interaction with our Father brings a reward.

Observe carefully what Jesus says. Again, He does not say that every prayer honestly directed to God will be answered. Experience has taught us that is not so. But every time we sincerely direct our prayer to the Father, there is a reward. This blessing is not based on the quality of our prayer, but simply as a response to our praying. The reward is not defined. Nevertheless, the promise is that we will be blessed. Our lives will improve every time we come to Him.

The Lord uses this example to illustrate the serious need to get past others and pray to God alone. We must not press the illustration further than He intended. Jesus did not go into closets to pray. He prayed in wilderness areas. That is how He got alone. Jesus also prayed in the presence of others. Later, group prayer would become a vital part of church life. Nevertheless, the principle remains, whether in private or in public: the essence of prayer is to get alone with God and direct our words to Him.

This is where Jesus starts in His teaching on prayer. It is where we must also start in our efforts to develop a healthy, accurate prayer life. By nature, all people have a profound tendency to live before men rather than before God. This tendency reveals itself in many ways. Some are similar to the man pictured in Jesus' first illustration. They love to pray in prayer meetings. There is nothing wrong with that. But all too often, that is the extent of their prayer lives. Apart from a group, they seldom pray; they need other people. Left alone with God, they are somewhat lost.

It shows up in other people as a desire to be known as men or women of prayer. They want their churches to be known as groups that pray. They want to encourage others to take up their places as prayer warriors. Although we should all learn to pray as well as possible, the reason we pray should not be to impress others with our commitment. The purpose of prayer is to get alone with God.

A more common manifestation of the tendency to pray to men is the fear of praying in public. Some avoid prayer meetings altogether. Others, trapped into public prayer, find their minds so blanketed by self-consciousness that they retreat to safe, generic prayer language to avoid potential embarrassment. To some extent, their fears of being judged are justified. We ourselves pass judgement on the prayers of others without even thinking about it. In the late 1960s when church life was very formal, I remember hearing a lady's account of the final day of a Bible conference she had attended. At the last session of the conference, the keynote speaker began his prayer, "Good morning, Dad." With those three simple words, the speaker divided the entire congregation. I suspect as you read what he said, you also had an opinion. We are kidding ourselves if we pretend that our prayers in public are not assessed.

I know every one of the tendencies I have spoken about because I have recognized them in my personal experience. These tendencies never disappear; we must guard against them and overcome them by a practical commitment of faith to what Jesus says. How can we overcome the pressure of public opinion and our own tendencies in order to learn to pray? Let me make some practical suggestions.

First, because the pressure of people is so strong, prayer must be learned in our alone place with God. Later, we will see the great value of God's people praying together. To be able to pray in a group, we must first master the principles of prayer on our own. Follow the Lord's direction. Find a place where you can go and know that you will not be observed. Because the pressure on our hearts to walk before people is so great, do not even let anyone know what you are doing. Make it a truly secret place.

Along that line, I would also strongly suggest that you do not take a cell phone with you. It is amazing how quickly the slightest evidence of an incoming communication can demand your attention. You have the privilege of spending time with the living God. For the short period you are with Him, give Him your undivided attention.

What should you do when you get to that alone space? My second suggestion is to never say anything until you are conscious of speaking to God. I have taught the Word of God for over forty years. A great deal of my own style of preparation involves formulating the plan. I do that by talking to myself. Well, not really to myself, but to an imagined group. Even as I write this, I picture people struggling to discover a meaningful prayer life. I write for them, even though they are not here. What does that have to do with prayer? Simply this, it is quite possible to completely get away from the physical presence of people and still formulate your prayers as if they were listening. For many, the habit of praying with people in mind is so engrained in them that they do not even recognize that they have not left those people outside the "inner room." When you get alone, do not say anything.

Think. Remember truth. You are in the presence of the God of the universe, and He is your Father, ready to hear your voice. The goal is not to achieve a sense of His presence. The objective is to bring your faith into conformity with this fact: God is already present and is listening. Jesus Christ said it is so; we must embrace the truth. We must not plow forward in prayer until we are taking hold of this grand reality.

Our Father is watching, and He is for us. We so often throw away truth and live in an emotional reality of our own creation. Then, we wonder why we do not experience the joy and peace God promises. People sometimes testify that when they pray, the heavens seem as brass. No doubt to them it may seem so, but it is not. Because of the work of Jesus Christ on a cross, that is not so. He died, the just for the unjust, to bring us to God (1 Pet. 3:18). The way to the holy presence of God is open. We may not sense His acceptance, but we have it, nonetheless.

It is sometimes said that it seemed as if a person's prayers were dead and never went higher than the ceiling. According to Jesus, they do not need to go higher than the ceiling. Our Father is there, in the room. He sees what is done in secret. Through Jesus Christ, we have access to Him, not because we can get to heaven, but because He has come near.

We are emotional creatures. We deal with an invisible God. The only way to know what is happening around us is to listen to what He has said. Begin your time alone with God by letting the Spirit of God bring your heart to faith. Do not speak until your mind is controlled by the truth of the Word. Keep this up when you come to pray, and after a while you will find that your immediate habit is to enter this mindset. Even in group prayer, your focus will be on the Lord Himself and not on those around you.

A third suggestion: never use prayer for any other purpose than to speak to God. I know the temptation here. Teaching the Word of God is an intense experience. Teachers speak for God Himself, and those who listen are in desperate need of interacting with Him. The mental shift from speaking to a congregation in a message to then addressing God in prayer at the end of a sermon poses a monumental challenge. I have often failed on this, so I am deeply sympathetic with all speakers who have finished their last point or recapped their entire sermon in their "prayer."

Perhaps you have sat with those who are grieving. You hurt with them and long to bring comfort to ease the pain and to start the healing. You pray with them. It is a simple slip to stop speaking to God and to begin recounting to them comforting words from Scripture, hoping to strengthen their faith. I recognize that such use of prayer would not fall under the same serious condemnation Jesus pronounces on those who pray to be seen by men. Those people have the praise of men as their reward. For preachers and counselors, the reward could be a good sermon completed or real, lasting comfort imparted. I tread softly here. The tendency to pray to people rather than to God is so strong that we must guard ourselves, even when the immediate result is beneficial. Prayer is for the purpose of speaking with God, not to preach, not to comfort, not to witness. Carry out all those activities with a whole heart. But stop when it is time to pray and to speak to God alone.

A final thought: stop assessing people's prayers. Even teaching prayer is difficult. A student looks to a teacher for instruction and for assessment of his progress. How can we do this when teaching a person to pray? If a conscientious student attempts to perform in his prayer as we have taught, we run the serious risk of training him to pray with his teacher in mind rather than God. I wonder how many revered leaders have unconsciously controlled the prayer development of others by granting or withholding an "amen". The pull of hypocrisy is strong. The prayers people pray are between them and their Father. Leave them there. This will not stop the problem of the flesh, but it will do two things. First, those who pray with you will begin to sense that their prayers are not on trial. If you help one person to shake free of praying before others, you have done a great service for the whole body. Second, you will find that if you stop analyzing the prayers of others, you yourself will find greater freedom to speak to God from your heart.

The essence of prayer is to get alone with the Father and in His powerful, understanding, and healing presence, to speak and to know the reward which comes from His wise, loving heart.

CHAPTER TWO

Your Father Knows

*And when you are praying, do not use meaningless
repetition as the Gentiles do,
for they suppose that they will be heard for their
many words.
So do not be like them; for your Father knows what you
need before you ask Him.*
Matthew 6:7-8

All men pray. It is a universal experience of the human race. As Christians, we sometimes find this difficult to accept. To be sure, we must broaden our definition of prayer a bit to recognize it, but it is true. If we are honest with ourselves, the even more disturbing reality is that the root of the prayers of those outside Christianity and of many inside Christianity are not all that different.

Two realities shared by all people guarantee that sooner or later everyone will resort to prayer. The first reality is that we were all made in the image of God. The second is that we must all live in a hostile world. Let's look at this more carefully.

God made mankind in His image. That image is stamped irrevocably on every heart. Sin and rebellion have twisted and marred that image, but it remains. His image gives each of us a significance that we all sense; we know our lives matter. By God's own design, we have been entrusted with enormous capacities. These enable us to think and to act like God. We are creative and protective. We organize and manage circumstances and people around us. Most importantly, we form relationships and increase our capacities through group activity. We develop and use all these capacities with the hope that they will lead us to a happiness which is something like the eternal joy in the heart of God.

Nobody dreams of failing or even of being average. Our godlikeness will not allow it. Think for a moment of the big dreams we had as kids. We wanted to be star athletes, renowned scholars, world-famous doctors, the president of the United States, or simply to be so wealthy that we could do whatever we wanted. We bounced from one dream to another, but all the dreams had one thing in common: our significance would be affirmed and we would be happy.

Sadly, there is a second reality. We live in a hostile world. On the one side, nature has not evenly distributed opportunity to people. We are not as intelligent or as attractive or as athletically gifted as others. On top of that, life confronts us with multiple dangers and obstacles. Disease, accidents, recessions, wars, climate change, and the list goes on and on. These factors are sprinkled randomly across mankind. They are not fair and they seem genuinely unjust, but we must face them, nonetheless. Then there is the other side. We find ourselves in a competition. Seven billion other people are trying to achieve the same kinds of dreams. In the competition, the field is not level and there is little we can do about it.

To handle the situation, we give it all we have. We do everything in our power to give ourselves an advantage. Then we employ others – family, teammates, coaches, business partners, gangs, cliques, whatever – to secure our end. Even then, we need help at times. When we have done everything we can and we have exploited every possible natural advantage, we still have need. So, we pray.

At times, this can look very humorous. Growing up as a baseball fan, I learned the sport has a tradition called a "rally cap". This appears when a team is behind in the late innings of a crucial game. With opportunity slipping away, grown men (gifted athletes, men who have spent countless hours honing their skills, members of professional organizations which have given them every opportunity to succeed) will turn their caps inside out or point them to the sky. Their hope is to somehow influence the "baseball gods" to give help. No one would claim they are serious, but they do it regardless. It is just the way people are.

Consider the lottery. At times, hundreds of millions of dollars are at stake. All a person can do to get a chance at that money, which they firmly believe will bring them happiness, is to buy the ticket. (I am not in any way advocating, simply observing.) On the day of the drawing, my strong suspicion is that many ticket holders will offer prayers. For some, it will be in the form of superstition – holding lucky objects, wearing lucky clothing, sitting in a lucky chair – all in an attempt to draw in any unseen forces that exist to tilt the odds in their favor. For others, it will be more formal. I wonder how many cases are made to God Himself as to why a certain individual should be given His help? I wonder further, how many bargains are made with the Almighty, offering to share the wealth with Him? For the overwhelming majority, their efforts will fail, and they will laugh them off. But their view of God and prayer will still be altered.

Sometimes the situation is not humorous at all. I grew up not far from the coal fields of West Virginia. Once, a mine shaft collapsed, trapping several miners deep within the earth. Recovery efforts were expected to be difficult and time consuming. While the rescuers labored, families in their community gathered in a local church. There they waited and prayed. I was very young, but the heaviness of my snapshot memory makes me believe that at least some of those men died. All men pray, but not all prayer achieves its goal. When it fails, their theology of God and of prayer often changes.

I know this was true for me. There was a phrase I heard from church members during my youth, "All we can do now is pray." And I knew that when all we could do for a sick person was pray, well, that meant he was going to die. We would pray because God could do something. After all, I had been told God could do anything. But I doubted it. I had heard stories of people who were healed in such circumstances. We called them "miracles." In my own heart, the miracle was not so much the display of power as it was a miracle that God did anything at all.

Again, I turn to another hazy memory of a television documentary I watched about a southeastern Asian country. In it, I remember a massive statue of Buddha surrounded by a large plaza. Around the base of the statue was a stone wall. People gathered at the wall and were placing small bits of paper in the crevices between the rocks. These were prayers they placed there in hope. The people came to the plaza with deep needs no different from our own, financial needs, health needs, family needs. Their fears and pains brought tears to their eyes. But the statue offered no comfort. He simply continued his stony stare out across the landscape. As Christians, we do not go to such images. But I fear that in times of crisis, the God to whom we pray often seems just as cold and unconcerned.

Jesus Christ knows our struggles with unanswered prayer. He is fully aware of the misconceptions of God that are created in our hearts by the trials of life and the whispers of demonic beings. He knew the crowd that assembled before Him that day. He used prayer to illustrate the need to walk before God, not men. But then He digressed. He had much more to say about prayer than simply coming to God. To pray without further insight into the unseen reality of God could lead to more hurt than good. Therefore, He addressed the way we should speak to God when we are in His presence. Let's listen to what He said. "And when you are praying, do not use meaningless repetition as the Gentiles do, for they suppose that they will be heard for their many words. So do not be like them; for your Father knows what you need before you ask Him" (Matt. 6:7-8).

The Lord's words could have easily stirred anger in the listeners. Do not pray like the Gentiles? The idea that there could be any comparison between the people of God and the heathen Roman world was absurd. Jews knew God; Gentiles did not. Jews had the covenant relationship; Romans and Greeks did not. But the warning was necessary. The whole human race, Jew and Gentile alike, shares a common uncertainty about the goodness of God. It is quite possible for our formal theology (what we boldly profess to believe) to have little or no effect on our practical theology (how we work out our relationship with God).

How do the Gentiles pray? Jesus says they use "meaningless repetition." That phrase is a single word in the Greek. Because it is a rare word, the exact meaning is debated. Some believe the emphasis is on the idea of babbling. The idea here would be to form a prayer from words which are used mindlessly. They come from a pre-scripted prayer rather than from the heart of the person. Others favor the concept of repeating words or phrases over and over. The New American Standard Bible combines the two thoughts and translates the word "meaningless repetitions."

Even if there is room for debate about the exact meaning of the word, Jesus clears up any question as to the motivation behind it. The reason He speaks against "meaningless repetitions" is because the petitioners believe they will be

21

heard for their many words. They believe that it is the length or the volume of their prayers that makes them effective. But why? Almost everyone would insist that an hour of prayer is surely better than five minutes, or that the longer prayer has more chance for success. Why is that so? Think again about our experience in prayer.

Most prayers seemingly go unanswered. Most people do not win the lottery or the national championship. Economic hardships continue; loved ones die; injustices go unpunished. But sometimes, prayer does produce results. Sometimes, we do see healing or find justice. Sometimes, our team does win. Stories of these "miracles" keep people praying. Why do some prayers work? If we do not listen to the Word of God, we tend to move towards one of two conclusions.

The first conclusion is that some people have stumbled onto the right words. They have found the secret formula, the secret words which move the unseen world. The emphasis is on correct expression. Say things the right way and God will listen; say them in the wrong way and He will ignore you. This leads to the use of prepackaged, formulated prayers to be recited at critical times. It may be very formal, as we find in a prayer book, or it may be that we simply use a prayer we have prayed before. If it worked once, why not say it again? Too many people believe that there is a magic formula or even a preferred language for coming to God.

The second conclusion is that God must be won over by a sheer barrage of words. Some believe that if they just keep praying long enough, they can pester God into submission. For others, the long prayers are just an attempt to get His attention as they call out from the seven billion person mob on this earth.

Both approaches have a common outlook: God is not interested in what takes place in our lives. We feel we have no vital connection. It is our responsibility to somehow get His attention, alert Him to our needs, and move Him to the point of concern. He is a busy God and our lives are not of much value. Sweet talk or barrage Him. If somehow you bother Him enough or hit the magic combination, He will take note.

The Lord gives us a completely different take on the nature of God. We do not need lots of words or secret formulas because the Living God is our Father. He is vitally concerned about our lives. He is so completely familiar with our situation that He knows our needs before we ever turn our attention to Him. To pray correctly, we must have a right view of the one to whom we come. Jesus' words challenge our attitude towards God in three areas.

First, far from being distant and aloof, we have a family relationship with God. He is our Father. As we will see in the next chapter, this is the relationship out of which effective prayer develops. True praying begins here.

Second, Jesus says that the Father knows what you need before you ask. God is omniscient. That means He knows everything, so of course, He knows our needs. But this "know" takes us beyond the realm of omniscience. This is the "know" of concern and genuine interest. God is not distant from His creation. Jesus says that He knows when even a sparrow dies, and people are worth a whole lot more than a sparrow to God (Matt. 10:29, 6:26). Paul says that even before we knew God, we lived and moved and had our existence in Him (Acts 17:28). Our Father knows. He knows because of His attention to who we are and what is happening in and around us. Think about what the Word of God declares concerning this. Listen to David in Psalm 139:1-4.

O Lord, You have searched me and known me.
You know when I sit down and when I rise up;

You understand my thought from afar.
You scrutinize my path and my lying down,
And are intimately acquainted with all my ways.
Even before there is a word on my tongue,
Behold, O Lord, You know it all.

When God speaks to us, He is never ignorant. He not only sees all, but He sees it from the perspective of a Father who is vitally interested in our wellbeing. Before we were born, He formed us. He watched us grow. He knows every advantage we have had and every obstacle we have had to overcome. He knows everyone who has loved us and everyone who has let us down. He knows all our sin and all the hurt that has been inflicted upon us. He knows every dream we have ever had, every motivation, every attitude, every fear, every unmet longing. Some of these thoughts were legitimate; some were crazy; some were sinful. But He knew them altogether. That is why the psalmist can say, "Even before there is a word on my tongue, behold, O Lord, You know it all" (Ps. 139:4). As I sit here and write and select words to express my mind, my Father knows everything that goes together genetically, educationally, emotionally, and in every other way to cause me to select one word as opposed to another. He was there when I learned each element of my vocabulary. He knows my patterns of thought and why they exist. What is true for me is true for every other person who reads these words.

Third, we must adjust our thinking about God because Jesus declared that our Father knows our needs before we ask. Our God is more than a passive observer. He lovingly knows everything that has happened to us to this point in our experience. But He also knows what we need. We do not ˑˑed to inform Him. We do not need to move Him. He has ˑʰere our lives have been. He knows what is ahead, not only in the near future, but also all the way to the end. In His loving care, He has made full provision for our lives.

In light of our Father's loving care for us and His constant attention to our lives, Jesus calls us to speak meaningfully to Him. We are not to harangue Him with words, as if He does not care. We do not need to hunt for some magic formula to gain an advantage. Prayer is honest, direct, heart communication between a believer and his loving Father.

What practical applications can we make to change the quality of our prayer experience? Real prayer is built upon a firm confidence in the goodness of God towards us, which flows from His love for us in Christ Jesus. We must never move from this confidence. It is the testimony of the Bible and we must embrace it by faith. "Jesus loves me, this I know, for the Bible tells me so." This is a children's chorus, but it holds great truth.

Ultimately, our understanding of the attitude of God toward us will develop from one of two sources. Sadly, most people formulate their opinion about God's love by the observation of human experience (particularly their own experience) interpreted to them by the god of this world. The alternative is to listen to the testimony of God through His Word. To find a rich experience in prayer, we must join the latter group. Bible teachers from my early experiences would say, "We must put a stake down on this." It is not enough to listen to the Word. We must do more than glory in the teaching about God's unspeakable love. We must embrace it by faith and act on it. There must come a point in time when we put our confidence in truth and make it the actual foundation of our living. That is what Jesus is talking about in the picture of the two houses at the end of the sermon: "Therefore everyone who hears these words of Mine and acts on them..." (Matt. 7:24). It is not enough to hear and understand. The capacity to face the storms of life here and to face the Lord in eternity will depend on building on God's Word.

I have a deep burden for this truth. I hear Bible teachers who, in an attempt to be transparent, speak about sometimes doubting the love of God. Let me be clear. There are times when we may not understand what God is doing. There will certainly be times when the path of God for our lives is uncomfortable and unwanted. Many saints have lived through terrible inward and outward suffering. These sufferings can lead us to ask the Father, "Why?" But we must never allow anything to rob us of the stabilizing truth that nothing can separate us from the love of God in Christ Jesus. Healthy praying particularly depends on this confidence.

Confidence in God's love for us is critical when we come to the topic of perseverance in prayer, which we will talk about in Chapter 7. We are asked to keep on praying. To some, this seems to contradict what Jesus says in Matthew 6. The Bible is not completely clear as to why we must ask repeatedly. But the Lord's words here remove one possible answer. Consistent asking is never necessary because God does not care or is not paying attention. Our ability to persevere in prayer depends on realizing we are working with God, not against Him, in prayer.

Then how should we speak when we come to God in prayer? Begin by facing this reality: before you ever say anything, your Father already knows your thoughts. One of the communion prayers, a prayer of confession from the prayer book I grew up with, starts, "Eternal God unto whom all hearts are open, all desires known and from whom no se-
's are hid...." Before you open your mouth, you need to
You cannot bluff God. You cannot butter Him up.
nide. He already knows everything in your mind.

He knows every longing. He observes every emotion. No matter what you bring to the prayer time, He is there ready to listen and able to meet. Speak honestly with God. That is always the first step to blessing.

This honesty does not imply arrogance. We are with God. He is the holy Father. But with honest humility in His presence, we can deal with anything. This place of fellowship with God is the only place where we can be perfectly honest and still perfectly safe.

Next, use meaningful words. Use the words that express your thoughts. "Emptiness" was part of the meaning of the words used by the Gentiles. There are no secret words. There are no formulas which make prayer work. God has no preferred language. We can get into trouble on this when we are first learning to pray. We listen to the prayers of seasoned saints and find it hard not to copy their phrases and patterns. We think, if God hears them, surely He will hear us if we pray like them. In the early days of my Christian life I was encouraged to take hymns, make them my own, and use them to worship God. This is a good practice if the hymns make sense to us. But even the words of Scripture fall short if we do not know what they mean. You do not need to develop a theological vocabulary to pray. No matter who you are, you have all the words you need. In time, as you learn more of the wonderful truth of God's Word, your vocabulary may change and your thoughts may expand. No matter where you are in your walk with God, use the words you understand to express the thoughts of your mind. We do not need to learn a new language to pray.

Let's take this a little deeper. While I sit here writing, moments of great frustration come. I cannot seem to put words together to accurately express what I want to say. When we are communicating with other people, this is quite important. We cannot read each other's minds. But when we come to our Father, this is never a problem. He knows our joys, hopes, longings, and pains more deeply than we ever will. He is touched by our weakness, even when we cannot express our thoughts.

Never use empty words in prayer. Speak to the person of God. The Lord is not saying that there will not be times when you will use a lot of words as you pray. There is a time to pour out your heart to the Lord. Some issues in life are complicated and painful; you just have to talk them out with your Father. You are free to stay as long as you want and to speak about anything that is on your heart. However, I would encourage you to stop when you have nothing left to say. Prayer is a discipline. When we first begin, we sometimes find it hard to come up with things to say. We hear about people who spend hours in prayer, so we try to imitate them. We set ourselves to pray for a certain amount of time. Let me encourage you not to do that. When you have run out, the danger is that you will start adding filler to keep going. If you are not careful, you can develop a prayer routine which enables you to keep your lips moving in prayer while your mind is somewhere else altogether. It is safer in the long run to come to the Lord, say what you have to say, and stop when you are finished.

One of the more common questions people ask is, "How do I deal with distractions?" You know what I mean. You start your prayer time with determination. You bring a list to stay on track. But your mind wanders as you pray. In the best-case scenario, you stop praying and start thinking. In the worst-case scenario, you keep uttering words or prayer formulas from past prayers. Your lips are saying one thing while your mind is saying something else. Then, when you catch yourself, you feel bad and try again, only to repeat the same pattern. What are you to do?

My suggestion is to pray about it. I do not mean you

should pray that the Lord will deliver you from distraction. There are strong indications in the book of Ezekiel that when we come to God, He listens to our hearts, not our words. The words are for us, to clarify our thinking. When we are distracted, our hearts are in the distraction. If that is what God is hearing anyway, why not bring it out into the open? Speak to God from your heart. If you have a concern keeping your mind occupied, talk to Him about it. If it is work that must be done, a relationship in which you are involved, a purchase you are considering, or even a leisure activity coming up, bring it to Him. You may learn a great deal about yourself in the experience. If you keep up the pattern, more and more of your life will be placed in His hands by faith, and your ability to concentrate on other matters in prayer will increase.

You have an unspeakable opportunity to get alone with God and speak to Him. His heart is towards you. He knows and understands your situation. He is ready and able to meet you in every way. You are safe in His presence. When you enter His presence, use meaningful words. Use your words to talk to your loving, heavenly Father.

CHAPTER THREE

Our Father

Pray, then, in this way: 'Our Father…'
Matthew 6:9

To whom are we speaking when we pray? The simplest answer to that question is "to God." In fact, for many, the very definition of prayer is "talking to God". But this does not help us very much in understanding prayer.

Imagine for a moment a man looking at his calendar and seeing that he has an appointment at 3 p.m. with a "human". That certainly does tell him something about the appointment. He will not be with a dog or a parrot. The time will be spent with a being who can think and talk and express emotion. A great deal could be said about what it means to be a human. However, unless the description goes further and says something about that person, how will the man prepare for the meeting? That person could be his boss. On the other hand, it could be his wife or grandchild or an IRS auditor. In each case, getting alone with the person would be a very different experience. It is all a question of relationship. Every time we meet a person, our interaction will be governed by the relationship we share. We learn in life to assess our relationships and to act accordingly.

At times, we can be in different relationships with the same person. Early in my life I worked for my dad's company. When I went to work for him, he did not stop being my dad. When I was at work, he was the boss. At home, the relationship was different. This becomes important as we begin to think about prayer. In that experience, we are alone with God. But what relationship governs our interaction?

As those who trust the revelation of God in the Scriptures, what can we say we know about Him? Certain characteristics are clear. He is a personal being. We can interact with Him. He is the all-powerful being. He is the God of perfect wisdom. He is supremely good, yet also infinitely holy. He is the Unchanging One who acts with unswerving purpose. He is the Faithful One. But how are we related to Him?

The Bible uses a variety of pictures to help us understand our connection to Him. Each is an illustration of a dimension of our experience with God. Think about a few of these significant concepts.

God is Creator. Everything was made by Him but also for Him. We are not free on this earth. He has the right over us, for we have life because of Him. He is the one to whom we owe everything.

God is pictured as King. Those in a right relationship with Him are subjects of His kingdom. In this respect, we are obligated to the laws and principles that govern His domain. Unfortunately, the illustration is somewhat impersonal. How much interaction does the average citizen have with a ruler? It is a relationship, but a bit distant.

Along a similar line, but becoming much more personal, He is pictured as the Master, while we are the servants. The idea of responsibility and obedience are maintained. The directives are received personally. Therefore, there is a direct and personal accountability to Him.

The picture of the head and the body describes how we share the Lord's life, carrying out His purposes in our daily living. Here, we are portrayed as those who do His will and express His character to those around us.

Then again, the Lord is the Shepherd. We are sheep. We are cared for, guided, and therefore know security in His powerful and wise activity on our behalf.

Moving to a relationship of greater intimacy, there is the picture of a husband and a wife. We serve the God of the universe in loving commitment. We have been conquered by love, not simply power.

When Jesus describes our approach to God in prayer, He uses a different illustration. "Pray, then, in this way: 'Our Father...'" (Matt. 6:9). The term "Father" is not new to our study. The essence of prayer is to get alone with God. But Jesus does not say "God". He says "Father". The Father is the one who sees in secret. We are to use meaningful language when we come, not simply because we have a God who knows about us, but because we have a loving Father. It is our Father who knows what we need before we ask. It is our Father who is constantly observing and lovingly working in our lives. In prayer, we come as children to our Father. Unless that realization forms the foundation of our praying, we will never realize what God intended for that experience.

Why did Jesus choose that relationship? We are not told directly, so I am speculating at this point. Think about it. This is one relationship we all have. If you are alive on this earth, you have a father. You may have had a wonderful experience, or you may have never known him. You may have only known him for a few years and been separated. You may have known him all your life and wish you had never met. But every one of us had a father. The problem with this is that our individual experiences are varied. Deficiencies in our own fathers may have warped our concept of the relationship. The complaint is legitimate and cannot be casually downplayed.

To address the issue, let's think first about those who had

"good" fathers. No matter how great our fathers are, they all miss the mark. None of them displayed the kind of love our heavenly Father has for us. Jesus speaks of this later in the Sermon on the Mount. Addressing the fathers in the crowd, He says that when their children ask for food, they supply it (Matt. 7:9-10). These are not the cruel, demented, twisted men that make the news for treating children like animals. Out of natural love, they provide for their children. And yet, He then says, "If you then, being evil, know how to give good gifts to your children, how much more will your Father who is in heaven give what is good to those who ask Him!" (Matt. 7:11). Even the best fathers are deficient. We must look somewhere else to fully understand our heavenly Father.

But what if your father was not even close to what he should have been? What if you were deserted or abused? The hurt that you experience is because you know he was wrong. You can detect the betrayal because, in your heart and mind, you know he should have been different. You know that the ideal is something way beyond what he displayed. But what is that ideal? You also need to look somewhere else to understand your relationship with God as His child.

Where should we look? We need to listen to what Jesus says. We need to know how the crowd that day would have understood a good father/child relationship. What came to mind when the word "father" was used among the Jews of Jesus' day? Two words help us to understand: security and significance.

First, let's think about security. Fathers were responsible to provide for and to protect the family. This is the most obvious point Jesus makes. It is also the easiest to see. Jewish people lived in a patriarchal society. For the most part, women were not in the work force. They worked hard, maybe even harder than their husbands, but all their labor centered on the daily needs of the family. Men worked to earn the money needed to supply the needs of the whole family. But their role was greater than that. A father also directed his family. He was responsible for the education of the children. Eventually, the choice of their spouses and the timing of their marriages was in his hands. Even after they were married, the father continued to look out for his children and grandchildren for the rest of his life. To have a wise, capable, and good father was a picture of security. As long as he was taking care of things, the children were free to use their energies for other matters.

But how does that work out? We cannot see God. We cannot look on His smile. And sadly, our whole nature has been conditioned to doubt God. In order to show us what the Father is like, God became flesh in the person of Jesus Christ. Jesus told His disciples that if they had seen Him, they had seen the Father (John 14:9). By watching Him, we know what the Father is like. And what do we see?

Jesus was *wise*. He answered every honest question. He met every person in exactly the way they needed. Nicodemus was totally different than the woman at the well. Jesus understood each one's needs and had exactly the right answer for them. He was never outmaneuvered by the trap questions of insincere people. Jesus knew exactly what to do in every circumstance. That is what our Father is like.

Jesus was also *capable*. He controlled the natural world. The deadly storm on the Sea of Galilee ended immediately at His command. A single meal became food for more than five thousand people at His creative touch. No disease was beyond His healing power. Death itself could not defy Him. In the political world, where men exercise power and authority, He was untouched until the moment He laid down His life. The Roman cross did not kill Him; when the time was right and His work was finished, He gave up His spirit to the Father. Even in the unseen realms of spiritual authority, He was Lord. Nothing successfully stood against Him. In all this, He showed us our Father.

But most important to the security of our hearts, Jesus was *good*. Jesus met the needs of everyone who honestly came to Him. He was kind to the wild demoniac from Gennesaret. He felt compassion on a widow who had just lost her only son. His heart was stirred as He confronted the isolation and pain of the leper. He was willing to heal. Even with the horror of crucifixion bearing down on Him, He reached out to the very cynical (but very needy) Pilate. When we watch His heart for people in need, we find out what the Father is like.

The word "Father" should bring us to security. If we entrust ourselves into His hands, the place of prayer should always be a place of peace. We often come with great burdens. To keep our spiritual balance, we must always come to Him as the all-wise, completely capable, and supremely good Father. Security is a powerful dimension in our relationship with God. Yet, if we limit our understanding of God as our Father to His loving care, we miss a great deal of the impact this relationship has on prayer.

Having the eternal God as our Father also defines the significance of our time here on earth. To understand this, we must consider the cultural difference between family life of the first century and our own American outlook. From my early years, I knew I was being prepared to be on my own. My parents had opinions as to what I should do with my life, but I knew that the final decision was mine. At one point in college, I was considering marriage. I introduced the young lady to my father and the three of us spent the evening together. After we took her back to the dorm, I asked him what he thought of her. Typical to the culture in which I was raised, his comment was simple. I was the one who would live with her, his opinion did not matter. This is probably extreme, even in American culture, but it is closer to our own outlook than anything the Roman culture contained.

In first-century culture, children worked for the family. Their education and their marriages were arranged by the father for the good of the family. Their place in society was tied to that family.

This seems an oppressive thought for us. We are taught to find significance by following our own dreams. The theme of countless movies is breaking free from the bondage of other people's opinions about what we should be and what we should do with our lives. We have to "be ourselves". Anything else destroys the possibility of happiness. For the determined and the richly talented, this may have an element of truth. For most of our culture, however, this outlook has led to terrible, secret insecurity. Too often, we do not know who we are or what we want. We cannot find a place where we fit.

To have a family in the Roman world meant to have immediate significance. Everyone in the group had a place. An orphan unattached to a family was viewed with pity. To have no family was to have no place. To be part of an important family was to have a significant life.

Although this aspect of family life is not detailed in the New Testament, the outworking of the concept is always there. During His early years, Jesus worked in a carpentry shop. The reason was simple. His father was a carpenter.

When Jesus called James and John to follow Him, they were in a fishing boat with their father. The seriousness of their decision was shown when they left their father in the boat. They deserted the family business.

Peter's father had apparently died. But that did not end the family experience. Peter and his brother Andrew continued to work together. It was the family business.

Paul affirmed the wholehearted ministry of Timothy. He served Paul just like a son would serve his father (Php. 2:22). Everyone would have understood the praise.

With that in mind, consider Jesus' outlook on His earthly life. Luke records a story when Jesus was only twelve (Luke 2:41-51). The family visited Jerusalem for the Passover then began their return trip. Even though His parents had not seen Jesus all day, they demonstrated the clan feature of life by assuming that He was with one of the relatives who traveled with them. When they could not locate Him, the distressed couple hurried back to Jerusalem and began a frantic search to find their son. When they found Him in the temple, speaking with religious teachers, He seemed surprised at their concern: "Did you not know that I had to be in My Father's house?" (Luke 2:49). The word "house" is better understood as "things." By Jewish standards, Jesus was now an adult. It was time for Him to serve His Father. And throughout the ministry He would later perform, He contended that everything He did was to please the Father. He was completely devoted to His Father's plan. Even in Gethsemane, He spoke to His Father of the abhorrence of what was to come. But the commitment was clear. "Not My will but Yours be done."

What does that have to do with us? A great deal. We are the children of God. This is true because of the new birth, but it is also true by adoption. Why would the New Testament speak of us as adopted children?

Roman adoption and Jewish adoption were slightly different, but no matter which culture the New Testament writers had in mind, the thought behind it was the same: to be adopted was a sign of honor. Consider the Romans. A Roman might have compassion on a child and raise him, but he would never *adopt* him while he was still a child. Adoption was a permanent arrangement. Natural children could be disinherited if they dishonored the family. Adopted children could not. A Roman would adopt an adult as an act of honor. He would bring the adopted son into the family to increase the prestige of the clan.

In the story *Ben Hur*, a Jewish aristocrat named Judah is reduced to a galley slave. During a sea battle, he saves a Roman admiral from drowning. The admiral recognizes Judah's character and capabilities and keeps him close to him in service. Eventually, he offers Judah the opportunity to be adopted into his family. He gives Judah a signet ring and the right to act on behalf of the family. That was Roman adoption.

In the Jewish world, things were a bit different. To them, adoption was the point in time when a natural son was recognized as a responsible member of the family. From that point forward, he would have adult standing in making decisions. He would have the right to act on behalf of the family. To Jews, adoption was an honor.

Consider the parable of the prodigal son (Luke 15:11-32). The young man acted privately. He severed ties, renounced his father, and dishonored his family. He traveled home in desperation and disgrace. Upon his return, the father showed his love by bringing him back as a son, not as a servant. The son's full acceptance was shown when he had the ring (the family signet) placed on his finger. He was restored to a place of honor. That is what our Father did for us when we came to Him. He gave us a place of significance.

This helps us understand why the New Testament would use the picture of adoption. To be forgiven is one matter. To immediately be given a place of responsibility is quite another. No wonder John would state in amazement, "See how great a love the Father has bestowed on us, that we would be called children of God; and such we are" (1 John 3:1). How can it be that we who once fought against the purposes of God could be given the right to act in His name? John also understood that to join the family of God, one has to renounce his former devil-headed clan. He told his listeners not to love the world or the things of the world (1 John 2:15). The reason is that if that love was there, they could not claim to have experienced the love of the Father.

When we come to pray, we come to speak with our Father. Since we are now in His family, the church and its affairs must become our primary concerns. This begins the moment we are converted and continues throughout our lives. The Father is creating circumstances in which every one of His children can exercise the authority of His name in order to advance His kingdom. Every day, our lives have a significance that those who do not know God cannot experience. No matter how important their work is now, it will disappear and lose all significance. No matter how insignificant our ministry seems in the family of God, even to the giving of a cup of water, it advances the Father's eternal plan. Prayer is a vital part of that work.

Before we move on from this consideration, let me address the question of Jesus Christ and the Spirit of God when we pray. Do we somehow forget the Lord Jesus as we come to pray? It is a legitimate question. First, let me remind you that there are no magic formulas in prayer. When we say that we pray to the Father, we are not suggesting that the prayer becomes useless if that title is not used. In Acts 4, the leaders of the church are praying in response to a threat from the Jewish authorities. They begin their prayer, "O Lord" (Acts 4:24). These leaders are not violating the teaching of the Lord Jesus. Jesus encourages us to come to prayer in light of our relationship with God as Father. But the person we address remains the Lord of all. He is also holy, faithful and loving. He is designated in the Scriptures by many different names, which broadens our understanding of His power and love. The disciples have been threatened by powerful government officials. They are simply reminding themselves that the one they know as Father is over every authority. We come to God as His children. In that relationship, we can glory in the greatness of any dimension of His being and trust Him to manifest His character in accordance to our need.

But what about Jesus Christ and the Spirit of God? Prayer is a fellowship with God Himself in all His fullness. We come to God as our Father. We are confident that we can address Him as such because the Son, Jesus Christ, has done a work on our behalf. We come on the basis of that work. Jesus is the one who brings us into the Father's presence. He is the priest that understands us and makes a way. He died, the just for the unjust, to bring us to God (1 Pet. 3:18). He is our access to the Father.

At the same time, the Spirit of God empowers us to pray. In the book of Ephesians, Paul encourages us to always pray in the Spirit (Eph. 6:18). The Spirit is our enabler in prayer. Each person of the Godhead is determined to see God's purpose brought to pass for mankind. In prayer, we are brought by the Son and we are empowered by the Spirit as we join the Father to see God's will accomplished. True prayer is a rich experience of fellowship with the living God.

CHAPTER FOUR

Seek First the Kingdom

Pray, then, in this way:
'Our Father who is in heaven,
Hallowed be Your name.
Your kingdom come.
Your will be done,
On earth as it is in heaven.
Give us this day our daily bread.
And forgive us our debts, as we also have
forgiven our debtors.
And do not lead us into temptation, but deliver us
from evil.
Matthew 6:9-13

We have considered some of Jesus' profound thoughts concerning true prayer from the Sermon on the Mount. The essence of real prayer is to get alone with the living God whom we can know as Father. Since that relationship over-shadows the entire interaction, there is no need for magic formulas or floods of words to gain His attention. He knows what we need and has considered that need before we ever come to Him.

Now the Lord turns to the content of our praying. "Pray, then, in this way" (Matt. 6:9). That should be good news to us. I remember the early days of my venture into the world of prayer. I knew prayer was important and that I should be praying more than I was. I got alone and determined to stay there for a set length of time. But I ran out of material very quickly. The Lord helps us with this problem.

The prayer Jesus outlines has commonly become known as the Lord's Prayer. How did He intend us to use this prayer? To answer that question, we should examine the prayers Jesus and His disciples pray in the rest of the New Testament. There is certainly no reason that we cannot pray the prayer as it stands. However, there is no record of anyone in the rest of the New Testament doing so. Therefore, we must conclude that the Lord's Prayer was never intended to be the "supreme" prayer or the only prayer to pray.

For that reason, the prayer is often called the *pattern prayer*. But there is still a problem with that idea. If we look at the various prayers that are offered in the rest of the New Testament, it is difficult to consistently show how they follow this as a pattern. Each contains elements of the concepts Jesus presents, but none follows the plan exactly. Maybe I am being a bit picky here, but I think the prayer should be understood, not as the pattern for our prayers, but as the perspective we should adopt as we come to pray. Not every New Testament prayer contains all the parts of the pattern given. At times prayers change the order of thought. But all the prayers recorded reflect a heart that has been shaped by the perspective of Jesus' teaching. To pray effectively demands purifying our outlook on life.

Ezekiel (chapters 8-11) records a vision the prophet received during a confusing period of Old Testament history. A godly king, Josiah, had led the nation in spiritual reform. Idols were destroyed, the temple repaired, and the priestly ministry restored. The people of God were once again giving themselves to the service of Jehovah. Yet Ezekiel predicted the destruction of Jerusalem and the temple as an act of God's judgment. The people of his day found that hard to understand. Part of Ezekiel's responsibility was to explain why this was happening. The vision of Ezekiel 8-11 gives us insight into the real nature of prayer. Ezekiel was transported to the temple in a vision to observe the worship of the nation from God's perspective. He saw the common worshipers, the leaders of the nation, and the priestly worship leaders. All of them were in the temple going through their prescribed rituals of worship. They did the right things and said the right words, but their actions and speech did not match their hearts. They worshiped God with their lips but longed for sin's pleasures and the sensual worship of idolatry. God heard their hearts, not their voices. The real prayer was what was going on in the depths of their inner being where the loving and the willing and the longings resided.

It is critical to understand the prayer Jesus presents as a heart perspective. The principles of prayer are not complicated to understand, but they are demanding to apply. To fulfill what Jesus is saying, a person must first change his heart perspective and then pray from that frame of reference.

We must study the Lord's Prayer in context of the entire Sermon on the Mount if we want to grasp its profound nature. The Lord introduces the subject of prayer to illustrate the danger of practicing righteousness to be seen by others rather than to honor God. What He says about how we should pray anticipates the next major point in the sermon. He states, "Where your treasure is, there your heart will be also" (Matt. 6:21). There are no exceptions to this principle because "No one can serve two masters" (Matt. 6:24). Jesus calls for a decisive action of the heart. "Seek first [as priority in your life] His [your Father's] kingdom and His righteousness" (Matt. 6:33).

Our ability to seek first the Father's kingdom rests on a point of faith. That point is the loving care of God in our lives. Life is difficult and dangerous. It was dangerous for the crowd that was present to hear the sermon Jesus gave. It is dangerous for us as we read over two thousand years later. All of us face economic dangers, health dangers, relational dangers, and social dangers. These are real issues that must be addressed. Now, here comes the point of faith. Our Father knows every need we have or ever will have, and He will meet each one perfectly. It is therefore safe to move our focus away from what we believe will give us security and joy. When we do that, our attention and energy are freed to advance our Father's purposes in this life. We can now safely devote ourselves to what we will refer to as the *family business*.

This same pattern of thought is found in the Lord's teaching on prayer. In Matthew 6:8, Jesus assures us that the Father, because of His great concern for us, knows our needs before we ask. If we do not keep returning to what He says about how to pray, we could conclude that our world and our happiness should be the main subject of our prayers. There are many religious teachers today that believe this. But the Lord goes in a completely different direction.

Because our lives are safe in the hands of a loving and powerful Father, we are released in prayer to give our attention to the advance of our Father's work in the lives around us. Imagine the way this would uplift the simple people on the hillside that day. From the perspective of the culture around them, their lives were of temporary value at best. But if they accepted Jesus' invitation, they could join the almighty God in doing a work that would last forever. The same opportunity is open to us, no matter who we are.

How should we pray? Proper perspective begins with acknowledging that we are speaking to "our Father who is in heaven" (Matt. 6:9). We have already considered God as our Father, but Jesus says that He is our Father in heaven. Literally, He is our Father who is in "the heavens". In the plural form "the heavens" contain at least three realms. First, there is the air we breathe and the atmosphere surrounding us. Second, there is the sky with the sun, moon, stars, and planets. And finally, there is the place where God dwells, the realm of perfection where God resides with the holy beings who always do His will. "Our Father, who is in the heavens" combines the two important concepts of transcendence and immanence. Transcendence refers to the superiority of God to anything we know. This would be an appropriate use of the word "awesome". In His power, goodness, love, and wisdom, He has no equal or competitor. If we saw Him as He is, we would be silenced by His greatness. The Father's immanence means that He is not aloof from this world. He is as close as the air we breathe. And further, He is active in that closeness. He is near to bless us.

Combined, these two concepts protect us as we pray. We need to see the grandeur of God in worship and praise, but we cannot forget the terrible need of people all around us. We must deal with the real issues of life in a fallen world while we are in God's presence, but we must not lose sight of the absolute control and delivering power of the one who sits on the throne. We come to our Father with the purpose that the family business may be advanced.

We should approach prayer with a sense of wonder. The Father has given us a chance to participate in the only work that will last. Our lives might seem mundane and our circumstances insignificant. But as we meet with our Father about those "insignificant" things, we influence them for all eternity.

There is a story about Sir Christopher Wren, the architect of the famous St. Paul's cathedral in London. One day when he went out to inspect the progress of the building, he came upon a group of men shaping stones for the great structure. He asked one worker what he was doing. The bored man looked at him as if it was the stupidest question he could possibly ask. "I am chiseling a stone," he said. Moving on to another worker doing exactly the same thing, the architect asked again, "What are you doing?" The man looked up and said with enthusiasm, "I am building a cathedral." No matter how limited our capacity, Jesus invites us to trust the Father concerning things that dominate everyday life and join the Father in completing His eternal plan.

What should our perspective be as we come to pray? Let's briefly look at the structure of what the Lord says. The prayer contains either 6 or 7 requests, depending on how we view the final section. Since the differences are not crucial, we will say there are six. Those six petitions are in two distinct groups of three each. The first three, listed in Matthew 6:9-10, are all aimed at the advance of God's plan on earth:

> 1) Hallowed be Your name (6:9).
> 2) Your kingdom come (6:10).
> 3) Your will be done, on earth as it is in heaven (6:10).

These first three requests all carry emphatic force. They are imperative (what we believe *must* happen). They represent the zeal of the intercessor as he comes before God. The second set of requests, found in Matthew 6:11-13, is not as strong. They relate to our own personal needs:

> 4) Give us this day our daily bread (6:11).
> 5) And forgive us our debts, as we also have forgiven our debtors (6:12).
> 6) And do not lead us into temptation, but deliver us from evil (6:13).

These petitions focus on necessary matters related to our weaknesses. They reflect our humility and dependence when we come to God in prayer. We need both zeal and humility when we pray.

Three petitions in the prayer focus on the plan of God on this earth. The request for God's will to be done, which finishes the first set, ends with the thought that it should be done here as it is done in heaven. Here the word "heaven" is singular, referring to the "realm beyond," where God resides. In that place, God is recognized for who He is. The glimpses we have into that reality picture a place of worship. The worship there arises from beings completely committed to honoring God by carrying out His beneficial and blessed purpose. The intercessor prays from a world separated from all that wonder. The driving force of prayer is the desire that the power of God should be experienced in a world filled with fear, frustration, and pain. We pray because it is possible for the curse people brought upon this planet to be broken by our Father's intervention. We keep on praying so that the healing grace of God will be seen in the faces of people with whom we interact daily.

The first imperative of the prayer is, "Hallowed be Your name" (Matt. 6:9). The Father *must* be held in the honor He deserves. In heaven, this is always true. Here on earth, it is not. Often, even those who desire to serve God have lost sight of who He is. It happened for Isaiah (Is. 6). He was loyal to Jehovah and had possibly even spoken for Him. But then a day came when He saw the Lord, and he was transformed. He learned who God was and, in that same instant, understood his own sin. Then he felt the wonder of cleansing and the grace of being included in God's purpose. Everything was permanently different once he saw the Lord.

The world is in trouble because it does not recognize God for who He is. That is not because the Lord is hiding. Each night, the starry canopy shouts to the human race that God exists. In Old Testament times, the Holy One cried out through prophets, kings, and historians. As a final revelation of Himself, He stepped into this world in the person of

Jesus Christ. All of this has been recorded and miraculously preserved, and it is available for anyone who wants to know Him. However, most of mankind does not honor Him. The devil, sin, and self-love have blinded people's hearts to Him. The name of God is used to curse as much as it is to seek Him. Jesus Christ, the only name by which blessing can come to people, is used as an expression of frustration or disgust.

The term "name" stands for the person. Jesus says that when we bow to pray, the central thrust of our requests should be that people would honor our Father for who He is in His person. We pray for the people we know in our families, neighborhoods, churches, and workplaces. All around us are individuals who are suffering in one way or another. They do not realize who God is and what He can do for them. The first petition tells us we should get before God and aggressively seek Him to change that deficiency in particular people.

This prayer is not only for those who do not know God. Obviously, if we are going to ask our Father for this to happen in the world, we must allow it to happen in us. This is often noted as the primary force of the prayer: "May I honor your name as it ought to be honored." To limit it to that thought is to rob it of the family aspect of the request. We pray to *our* Father, not just *my* Father. The family business is the glorification of Jesus Christ. All of God's plan is moving towards a moment when the Lord will be recognized for who He is, and His saving work will be put on display. In that day, the church He has built will be to the praise of the glory of His grace (Eph. 1:6, 12). In the grace of God, those of us who have been made His children participate in that plan. For all the children of the Father, the first imperative is that His name must be held in honor in men's hearts.

Jesus goes on to a second imperative: "Your kingdom come" (Matt. 6:10). The kingdom of God *must* come. In heaven, God is recognized as the Ruler. Isaiah saw Him sitting on a throne, actively ruling (Is. 6:1). Jesus became a man so that the kingdom of God might come on earth. God has a plan and that plan is moving steadily towards a goal. One day, on this earth, every created being will bow and acknowledge Jesus as Ruler.

Today it is not so. The commands of the King are either aggressively or ignorantly set aside. Our Father is still King, but, at this moment, His right to rule is challenged. Today the kingdom of God comes to individual hearts. It comes when a person actively submits to the purpose of the King; it comes when His right to rule is accepted.

Evangelism naturally follows when these first two imperatives govern our inner lives. People do not recognize who God is and therefore will not submit to Him. That *must* change. Our Father must be honored for who He is. There is no alternative. He must rule in the hearts of the real people He created for Himself. These must come to the place of repentance and faith, which will lead to His rule in their hearts.

This is also the force of prayer for the church. The people who claim to know Christ must fully understand who He is. That is what Paul was asking when he prayed "that the God of our Lord Jesus Christ, the Father of glory, may give to you a spirit of wisdom and of revelation in the knowledge of Him" (Eph. 1:17). They also needed to live by kingdom principles, so Paul prayed again that they would be strengthened by the Spirit of God to manifest faith and love (Eph. 3:14-19). According to Philippians 3, Paul's personal desire was to fully know the Lord, but his burden did not stop there. It was imperative that the whole church come into that experience. That is the end he worked towards; that is the end he prayed towards.

All this must become very practical. The desire for the name of God to be honored and His rule to be extended must never become a generic daydream. When Paul prayed for the Ephesians, he was thinking of people he knew. He knew their background. He understood the misconceptions and pressures that limited their faith and love. He prayed for people with faces. The same must be true for us. Our Father has not given us the responsibility to take the gospel to the whole world. That is the goal for the church as a whole, but it is completely unrealistic for us as individuals. However, He has given each of us a realm of influence at this very moment. We have families; we live in communities; we fellowship with groups of believers; we have circles of friends. These imperatives touch them. Our children, parents, and siblings must honor the Father and follow Him as Lord. Our church must know who God is in an ever-increasing manner. They must see the truth of God clearly and embrace His purpose wholeheartedly. Our neighbors must comprehend the beauty and power of God. They must come to the King in an act of committing faith. Our world might not seem very large, but when we come to pray, we come to ask God to work so that people's ignorance of God and their bondage which comes from refusing His rule would be broken among these people.

Do you remember those days when you had so little to pray about that you could not fill up five minutes? Once we stop focusing on our own little world and join the Lord in His plan for people, we will not question how to fill up our prayer time. We will work to hone our prayer skills to cover the incredible opportunities all around us.

The final imperative of the first set is, "Your will be done on earth as it is in heaven" (Matt. 6:10). The will of the Father *must* be done. Similar words occur with different meanings in other parts of the New Testament. Jesus was repulsed by the horror of what would occur in the experience of the cross. As a man, He did not want to face it. But He was the servant of His Father and submitted to His will with the words, "not My will, but Yours be done" (Luke 22:42). This was a beautiful act of submission, but it does not express what Jesus is teaching here. When Paul received word that he would be imprisoned when he went to Jerusalem, His friends took it as a warning not to go (Acts 21:12). Paul understood it as a preparation for what was about to take place. When it became clear that Paul could not be persuaded, the rest said, "The will of the Lord be done" (Acts 21:14). They had resigned themselves in faith to the leadership of Paul. It was a healthy response when they could not change the circumstance, but it is not what Jesus is saying here. There is no sign of resignation in this petition. The petition is an insistence that God's will be done despite any opposition which may come.

Our desire is that everyone come into the kingdom of God. That will not come to pass. This request deals with those places where people do not have any intention of following God. Some who refuse have a great deal of influence over what happens in our lives. Often, we have no control over their actions. If the purpose of God is to be done on this earth, He must exert His authority where individuals or groups oppose Him. The devil is the god of this world. This petition is a cry to the Lord to intervene to thwart his plans.

The request is not limited to situations involving open opposition. How many government decisions are made that affect our everyday lives? I doubt that many are made to purposely hinder God's people. They are just decisions. For many years, international students have come to the discipleship school in which I teach. They need visas to get into the United States. Part of that process involves going to the embassy in their country and answering questions about their situation. The officials who interview them have almost unlimited authority to grant or withhold permission to come. Some may openly oppose Christianity. Others are probably completely neutral. When they make the trip to the embassy, we must pray that the will of God be done.

We said earlier that these three requests are the passion of our praying. Our God must be honored for who He is. His kingdom must come in the hearts of men and women. His will must prevail, even when there is no heart submission. In the fallen state of this world, where so many forces oppose Him, we pray that our Father would sovereignly control in the same way He rules in heaven, where everyone and everything supports Him. The family business absolutely must be advanced.

The second part of the prayer is dominated by an understanding of our weaknesses and limitations in our service to God. It reflects the humility that characterizes a true child of God. These petitions are supportive of the first set. Think of those first disciples who received a commission to go into all the world and make disciples. They were zealous to go; they had good news to deliver. But as Paul puts it, the treasure was in an earthen vessel, a simple clay pot (2 Cor. 4:7). These petitions relate to the daily care of the vessel.

I would start with the word "daily". There is some debate about the exact meaning of the word, but commentators agree that it brings us into short-term thinking about our lives. These requests are for the immediate present. As we have seen, this is the only place where God works. He is the ever-present I Am. The kingdom of God is coming right now. To stay in step with the eternal God, we must learn to function in the immediate present.

Living well in the present is not an American strong point. We live in an achievement culture. In order to achieve, we plan. There is nothing wrong with planning. But there is a fine line between planning for the future and living there. As a culture, we are not comfortable with the present. We live for the weekend or for our next vacation or job advancement. When stuck in the present, we retreat to entertainment, cell phones, or video games. The problem is not the entertainment or the vacations. The problem is that too often our preoccupation makes us oblivious to the real-time needs of those around us. I know how this works. I know what it is to be so concerned about the future of the work of God that I am not available to the people right in my presence. I have often been rebuked by this feature of the Lord's work. He was always able to give Himself to the people around Him. Hours before the agony of the cross, He sat peacefully with His followers to comfort and to prepare them for what was ahead. He was centered in the immediate present.

Our Father must be honored today. His kingdom must be advanced today. His will must be done in the uncontrollable circumstances we face today. One of the best pieces of advice I received in my early Christian life was, "Learn to live well in the immediate present." All we really have is today. But here is the most wonderful of truths. We can do the family business for the honor of our Father no matter what our "today" holds.

Jesus sums up our daily needs in three petitions. We need daily provision which comes from our Father. Next, we need the daily experience of forgiveness. Finally, we must have daily protection, which only our Father can provide.

The first daily need we have is provision. The Lord reduces all our various needs to a single statement: "Give us this day our daily bread" (Matt. 6:11). "Bread" here should be taken to represent all the daily necessities for life. We are not little gods. We are not superhuman beings. To keep on going, we need a continual supply line. Our Father knows what we need before we ask. But we are still called to come and ask. We are totally dependent creatures and are told to daily acknowledge that dependence.

Obviously, every kind of physical provision would be included in this petition. We need food. But we also need clothes and housing and health care and education and a whole host of other things. Typically, the Father will supply our needs by giving us means to provide for ourselves. We need jobs and health to work those jobs. All of this would come under the idea of receiving daily bread.

But our physical needs do not exhaust the daily needs of our hearts. In Luke 11:9-13, the Lord is arguing the need to continue steadfast in prayer. He says that even earthly fathers provide food for their hungry children. In an unexpected twist, He says, "How much more will your heavenly Father give the Holy Spirit to those who ask Him?" (Luke 11:13). Spiritual supply is likened to meeting biological hunger. If we are going to do the family business in an effective manner, we will need much more than physical provision. We need wisdom, emotional strength, companionship, and spiritual enabling. Paul puts it this way: do not be anxious for anything; pray about everything (Php. 4:6). We should not allow the anxiety which comes from an unmet need to remain in our experience. We should bring it to our Father and count on His loving provision.

The second daily need we all have is forgiveness: "And forgive us our debts, as we also have forgiven our debtors"

(Matt. 6:12). Note that the petition is conditional: *forgive us in exactly the same way we have forgiven others*. We have need of the Lord's forgiveness; people around us have need of our forgiveness. Jesus will come back to this point, and we will look at it in more detail in the next chapter. Suffice to say here that the family business is carried out among less than perfect people. We will face both temptation and opposition. Sadly, we will fail to be what we should be. We will sin and others will sin against us. Healthy spiritual living depends on seeking the Lord's forgiveness and granting forgiveness to others on a daily basis.

Finally, we have the daily need for safety: "And do not lead us into temptation, but deliver us from evil" (Matt. 6:13). Some see this section as containing two different petitions. The first is to be kept from temptation, the second is to be kept from evil. We will sum up the two under the thought of protection.

"Go therefore and make disciples of all the nations" (Matt. 28:19). That is what the Lord tells us to do. Yet from the beginning of the church's experience, it has been a problem. As representatives of Christ and the family of God, we have a responsibility to display a Christ-like character. Culture does not help in achieving that goal. We are called to be pure in a filthy world. We must be honest in a deceptive world. We must be generous in a greedy world. We need to show love in a brutal world. We face real pressure every day. In response, we feel enticed to avoid the pressure by retreating. Yet we know we cannot go there. We have been given a job to do. God's name must be honored. People must be brought into the kingdom of God. And people who know the Lord must be built up to serve. We must go out. The honoring of God, the coming of His kingdom, and the doing of His will all depend on the church moving into cultures, no matter how corrupt those cultures are.

Going out inevitably leads to two results. First, we are exposed to the sinful tendencies of those to whom we go. The worst part of that exposure is that we realize there is a problem in our own beings which pulls us towards the same conduct. As the church moves out to accomplish the purpose of God, we need to ask the Father to shield us from temptation. God does not tempt anyone to sin. The request does not imply that He will send temptation if we do not ask. It is an appeal to the Father to remember our weakness as we seek to fulfill His will for our lives, and to protect us from unnecessary and overwhelming temptation. I have listened to people pray for over forty years. I am surprised at how seldom this prayer is made. I have often wondered how much failure of character among church leaders is simply the result of not recognizing our weakness and consistently asking for protection.

Temptation is not the only area in which we need protection. One of the more alarming biblical studies to make is to consider the responses of people to Jesus Himself. He was never unkind, never aloof. With very rare exceptions, He met every request for help which was made. Late in His ministry, He raised Lazarus from the dead. And Lazarus was very dead. In response to this glorious demonstration of His authority over our greatest enemy, the religious leaders left the scene to plot Jesus' death. Human pride, fueled by Satanic antagonism to the things of God, guarantees that those who go into the world will face difficulties. As Paul says, "Indeed, all who desire to live godly in Christ Jesus will be persecuted" (2 Tim. 3:12). We should avoid words and actions that artificially fuel conflict, but no matter how loving and giving we are to those around us, we cannot avoid contention. Jesus encourages us to make it our daily prayer to be kept from evil.

The word "evil" could be either the devil as the evil

one or the circumstances which have an evil effect. Either translation puts this in a different category than the suffering which is common to all people. The emphasis is on the way in which the devil can use circumstances to rob, kill, and destroy.

We are not praying to be kept from difficulties or suffering. As much as we dislike experiencing pain of any kind, it often gives us a platform to speak about our faith in God. In suffering, the Lord often demonstrates His greatness to us and to others. At other times, the same suffering deepens our understanding and compassion, enabling us to relate to others and to tell them of the grace of our Father. The prayer Jesus encourages us to pray daily is that the Father will not allow our enemy to use difficult circumstances to accomplish his destructive purposes.

Now let's step back and ask some hard questions. How do we pray? If there is a zeal to our praying, what drives that zeal? If we wrote down the things we have asked of our Father over the last week, how would they compare with this prayer? An inspiring young couple recently spoke to the students of the school where I work. Along with their children, this couple ministers to refugees in the Middle East. From the perspective of the United States, the work is dangerous. On several occasions, they have found themselves in the middle of military conflict. When they listed their prayer requests, however, they asked us not to concentrate on safety. "We have enough people praying for our safety. We are not in this work to stay safe. We are there so that, by any means the Lord chooses, we can make Christ known." They had picked up the spirit of the Lord's Prayer. This is a bit of a watershed issue. This is what separates Christian praying from the prayers of those who do not really know God. If God answered our prayers, how much would the kingdom of God be advanced? To pray effectively, the passion of our hearts must become the advance of the kingdom of God. When that is true, powerful changes take place through our time with the Father.

In concluding this section, it might be helpful to see this in action. The book of Acts makes it clear that the early church prayed regularly. But the Spirit of God has not given us many insights into the precise content of their prayers. A notable exception is found in Acts 4:23-31.

To set the scene, Peter and John had been dragged before the religious council of Jerusalem. This was the group of very powerful and zealous men who engineered the crucifixion of Jesus. A tense confrontation ended with an order not to speak to anyone in the name of Jesus. This, of course, was impossible for them to obey. Jesus specifically told them to testify everywhere about Him. After further threats, they were released and immediately went to speak to the church leadership about the confrontation. We do not know exactly who was in the group, but we can assume that many had families, jobs, and homes. The threats against them were threats against everyone with whom they were associated. What is the right way to pray in a dangerous situation like this?

First, notice that there was one mind in the group about what they needed. This group, to the person, was committed to the Lord. They prayed to the Father who is in heaven. They called him "Lord" in the prayer, reminding us again that "Father" is not a magic word but a relationship from which we pray. Two facts about His Lordship encouraged them. First, everything that exists is the work of His hands and, therefore, under His control. Second, they affirmed their confidence that everything evil carried out by the Sanhedrin against Jesus Christ was actually and finally controlled, even ordered, by the Father to promote His saving purpose. They could trust their God in a dangerous place.

Three petitions then rolled seamlessly from their hearts. First, "take note of their threats" (Acts 4:29). They recognized that He was God; they were His creatures. Ultimately, they were in His hands; their confidence was that He would be in control, whatever the outcome. Second, and most important, they asked for the provision they needed that day: "Grant that Your bond-servants may speak Your word with all confidence..." He told them to speak in His name. To do that, they needed strength to speak the message He gave them with confidence. Then finally, they asked the Lord to act in such a way that people would recognize His greatness and promote the glory of Jesus (Acts 4:30). In the face of serious danger, they sought first, as a matter of priority, the kingdom of God.

The approving and confirming response of God is stunning. When they finished, the Father shook the room in loving assurance of His approval of the prayer. Then, they were all filled with the Spirit of God. He granted them strength by His Spirit; they went out and spoke the message of God boldly. The church was sacrificially unified, continuing to grow in size and purity.

We have bold access to a loving heavenly Father. Because He is looking out for us, we are released in prayer to seek, as priority, His kingdom and His righteousness.

Section Two:

Preparing for Prayer

CHAPTER FIVE

When You Pray, Forgive

*For if you forgive others for their transgressions, your
heavenly Father will also forgive you.
But if you do not forgive others, then your Father will
not forgive your transgressions.*
Matthew 6:14-15

*Whenever you stand praying, forgive, if you have
anything against anyone,
so that your Father who is in heaven will also forgive
you your transgressions.*
Mark 11:25

The fifth petition of the Lord's Prayer is an appeal for
forgiveness. Forgiveness is a beautiful and healing word.
The root meaning of the verb is "to send away." When used
concerning monetary debt, it means to take the debt off the
record. There is cancelation; the responsibility of repayment
is completely removed. In a similar way, when it is applied
to the problem of sin, it declares that the offense is taken off
the record. With its removal from the record, the offender
is delivered from the penalty the sin deserves. Everything
to this point in our consideration of prayer depends on the
fact that, through the death of Jesus Christ on the cross, our
Father can deal with us as if we had never sinned. Because
of Jesus' sacrifice, the Father can meet with any honest seek-
er. Because of His work, we can know God as Father and
approach Him at any time. Because the guilt of our sin has
been sent away, we can join our Father in His great work.

God's forgiving work in Christ lays the foundation for all healthy fellowship with the Father.

Receiving forgiveness changes our outlook towards others and their mistreatment of us. Receiving forgiveness from the Father and our willingness to grant forgiveness to others are vitally linked. According to the Lord, a forgiving spirit is also tied to our prayer experience.

When Jesus completed His presentation of the essential elements of prayer, He commented on the fifth petition. He wanted to underline the way in which He worded that request. Asking God to forgive us is probably one of the more common forms of prayer. It would seem to be a rather straightforward request, but Jesus adds a twist. He links our experience of forgiveness to our willingness to forgive. For the Lord, this is a crucial matter. The subject of our study is prayer, not forgiveness. Yet, three times in the Gospels, prayer and forgiveness are found together. The Gospel writers obviously saw a connection between the two.

Matthew 6:14-15 is the earliest passage where this combination occurs. In the prayer the wording is "And forgive us our debts, as we also have forgiven our debtors" (Matt. 6:12). The Lord likens our sin to a debt that must be paid. The request is that the Father would send it away, that He would remove it from the record. This is more than a technicality. Every sin is an offense to God. It creates a debt that clouds our free fellowship with the Father. In Christ, we receive complete forgiveness. Since we fail to live as we should on a daily basis, we need to be daily washed to keep fellowship with our God free and open. Dealing with sin daily should be the habit of every child of God.

Although prayer for forgiveness is one of the most common forms of prayer, the Lord adds a condition, which is seldom part of our praying, to the request. He tells us to ask the Father to forgive us in exactly the same way as we are forgiving others. The request for personal forgiveness must be made from a generously forgiving heart.

Just to be sure we do not miss the importance of what He is saying, the Master returns to this subject. Note that there is a change in the word for sin. In verse 12, He uses the word "debt". That word emphasizes the thought that when sin occurs, something is owed; a debt must be paid. We owe God because of our sin. Others owe us because of their sin. In both cases, there is the need for forgiveness to send those debts away and to clear the record. In verses 14 and 15, He uses the word "transgression". The word's basic meaning is to make a false step, to blunder into a place we should not have been. This is what happens when we sin. God's Word gives us a roadmap for life; it shows us the path. When sin causes us to take false steps, we stumble off the path, offending God. The same concept can be applied to our interpersonal relationships. There is a path of kindness, generosity, and honor that keeps our relationships with others peaceful. At times, we make false steps that cause offense and result in hurt and division. These are the transgressions the Lord has in mind.

Returning to the teaching on forgiveness, Jesus focuses on the intercessor's relationship with the people around him. Listen to His words: "For if you forgive others for their transgressions, your heavenly Father will also forgive you. But if you do not forgive others, then your Father will not forgive your transgressions" (Matt. 6:14-15). Our forgiveness is linked to a determination to forgive others when we have been offended. The Lord is telling His listeners that we cannot separate the two.

To understand the Lord's outlook on this matter, we

should consider the second passage where the teaching on prayer and forgiveness are connected. It is found in Matthew 18. The entire chapter focuses on the importance we should place on our relationships with others, particularly those in the family of God. In verse 6, He speaks of the danger of acting in ways that cause little ones to stumble from God's path. Whether He is speaking of literal children or of those young in the faith is debated, but the emphasis is on the weighty responsibility each of us has to look out for their welfare. We must never look down on these young ones; we must protect them.

He then turns to the subject of how every lost sheep is important to God. Lost sheep are people who have wandered from God into sinful and unhealthy living. He does not want even one of these "little ones" to be lost. Continuing that thought, Jesus encourages us to make every effort to influence a person who has stepped aside from God to return to Him. The goal of this disciplinary process is to "win your brother". Your brothers and sisters are important.

He then turns to the great authority the church will have on earth. That leads to a great promise on prayer, which we will consider in Chapter 9. "Again I say to you, that if two of you agree on earth about anything that they may ask, it shall be done for them by My Father who is in heaven" (Matt. 18:19). Where even two or three are gathered in His name, He is right there with them. Unity in the church leads to power in prayer.

Matthew 18:21 begins with "then". William Hendriksen says that "then" keeps the following question in close time sequence to what has just been said.[1] The immediate context is prayer; the larger context is the importance of the body of believers. Unity is a wonderful concept, but anyone who has tried to keep the peace in a family, in a church, on a jobsite, or anywhere else knows that conflicts and offenses are inevitable. Keeping peace is hard work, which requires a forgiving spirit. Peter asks for guidance on how far to take this. When can I say "enough is enough"?

Listen to Peter's generous offer. "Lord, how often shall my brother sin against me and I forgive him? Up to seven times [a number of perfection]?" The implication is not simply seven different offenses. How many times must we forgive a person for the same kind of offense? How much do we have to take from difficult people? Peter is quite generous about this. Forgiving a person who has hurt us the same way seven consecutive times would be considered by almost anyone (with the possible exception of the offender) as more than adequate, actually quite noble. Peter's question implies that there must be a limit. There must be some point at which we are justified in withholding kindness and sealing that person out of our hearts.

However, Jesus replies, "I do not say to you, up to seven times, but up to seventy times seven" (Matt. 18:22). Jesus' well-known response is not just an attempt to raise the bar to a larger number before a person is considered unforgivable. The number he gives indicates that forgiveness is an outlook that must become part of our constant approach to all people.

To illustrate the point, He gives a parable. It opens with a heartbreaking scene. The steward of a king has gotten himself into hopeless debt. The amount is 10,000 talents. It is estimated that it would take an average worker 15-20 years to earn one talent. Multiply that by 10,000 and you get the picture of how extreme his dilemma was. The man pleads for time to repay. Although that is impossible, what else can he do? His family is about to be split up and sold into slavery. All he owns will be taken. His name will be utterly disgraced. His plea moves the king. In an act of supreme kindness, the king forgives (sends away) his steward's debt. It is all removed from the record; He no longer has to pay. His deliverance is complete. What a wonderful illustration of the grace of God towards us as offenders of His law.

The beautiful picture quickly becomes marred. The forgiven steward finds a man who owes him money. He may have sought out the debtor or just run into him, but he was there, nonetheless. The debt was small and payable ($1/500,000^{th}$ of what had just been forgiven). The man makes the same appeal that the steward himself made to the king. The steward's response is tragically different. The plea is ignored, and the man is thrown into prison.

Hearing of this turn of events, the king reverses his decision. The ungrateful steward is turned over to be tortured until he pays all. That will never happen; the debt is just too large.

Jesus makes a simple application. This is what will happen to everyone who does not forgive his brother from the heart. He is not teaching that we can earn salvation by having a forgiving spirit. The point is that if we cannot forgive others, we have never understood the magnanimous grace of God. We have never really experienced God's forgiveness. Forgiveness is essential to following Jesus.

This is a most important aspect of our relationship with Jesus. There are too many who claim to have experienced the grace of God yet still hold unforgiveness in their hearts towards people on this earth. How many church splits occur precisely because members cannot forgive each other? How much of the constant parade of believers from church to church is the result of wounds that they think can be cured by escaping interaction with the offenders? How many Christian homes are split apart by the pressure of resentment over mistakes? Jesus speaks to us bluntly because He came to set us free. As long as our hearts are controlled by the hurts of the past, we are bound. What is more, these hurts indicate that we have never taken hold of the forgiving grace of God in Christ Jesus.

Practically, what does this teach us concerning our prayer experience? To answer that, let's turn to a final passage on the connection of prayer and forgiveness in Mark 11:22-25. It was late in the life of the Lord. Jesus was in Jerusalem for the final week of His ministry. The city was packed with pilgrims for the Passover celebration. Jesus and the disciples had a place to stay outside the city itself. As the band of disciples walked to the city one morning, Jesus saw a fig tree by the road. He was hungry and looked for some fruit. Finding none, He cursed the tree. The act was symbolic. It was also dramatic. The tree withered from the roots upward. Peter, still amazed by this event, commented on it the next day as they passed the shriveled bush. Jesus took the opportunity to speak to His followers about prayer and faith. First, if they had faith, mountains would move at their word (Mark 11:23). Then He moved to prayer. Prayers offered in faith would always be answered. These are powerful thoughts which we will consider later.

At this point, the teaching on prayer takes an unexpected turn. Jesus moves from faith in prayer to forgiveness. "Whenever you stand praying, forgive, if you have anything against anyone, so that your Father who is in heaven will also forgive you your transgressions" (Mark 11:25). The link between our forgiveness and God's forgiveness is the same. However, here the Lord tells us what we should do about that. There are four key words in His instruction: whenever, forgive, anything, and anyone.

First, *whenever*. "Whenever you stand praying, forgive" (Mark 11:25). Standing was the typical posture for prayer in Jesus' day. We would probably say it this way, "Whenever you kneel to pray..." It means every time we pray, when we approach God, there is something to do. We must do it every time, on the spot. This point is important.

The second important word is *forgive*. That is what we are to do every time we come to pray. What does He mean? Note first that He is speaking of forgiveness, not reconciliation. Forgiveness is a prerequisite to reconciliation, but the two are different. Forgiveness, as Jesus uses the term here, is something that happens in our own hearts. It is between us and the Father. Reconciliation is between us and another person. It is the practical healing of a broken relationship. We should be ready to extend forgiveness to anyone who asks for it. We certainly should actively work to reconcile relationships which have been harmed. Jesus is not speaking here of something between people, but something that happens in the heart of the person who has come to pray. Right there, on the spot, he is to forgive and then go on with the prayer. Note that this instruction is very different from the one found in Matthew 5:23. There He speaks of making an offering when you know that someone has something against you. In that case, you are the person who has caused the hurt. You have caused a break in fellowship with someone because of your offensive behavior. In that situation, He calls us to stop the offering until the relationship has been restored. Relationships are more important than offerings.

But in Mark 11:25, you are the one who has been offended. The offense has caused some degree of bitterness. When you stand to pray, Jesus says to deal with the bitterness, send it away, clear the record. The need is in your own heart and can only be met as you let go in an act of forgiveness. When you have done that, you are prepared to join the Father in His work of bringing the good news of forgiveness in Christ to people around you.

Then there is the word *anything*. The forgiveness is to

be extended to every kind of offense that you may have experienced. Three areas need to be mentioned at this point. First, there are the devastating kinds of offenses which leave permanent damage in our lives. We live in a day in which one in five children has been abused in serious ways. Those abuses will leave permanent results. It is easy to look at these offenses as if they are beyond the possibility of forgiveness. Jesus says *anything*, no matter how large.

Then there are the petty offenses, those little annoyances which we experience every day. In a sense, we pass them off, but they need to be addressed. Major relational problems often have their source in a collection of unresolved and unforgiven offenses that have been accumulating in the heart and the mind. As a matter of spiritual hygiene, each time you prepare to pray, stop and clear all those issues before God.

Then finally, note that Jesus does not mention the word *sin* here. He is not concerned about whether we were really wronged or not. If there is a perceived offense, forgive it. This would go a long way towards promoting Christian unity. This is particularly important in a society which searches to find offense in even the most inoffensive actions. Meaning is assigned to actions that have no meaning. Imagination embellishes a look or a word into an attack. How many serious church conflicts are the result of misunderstood or misrepresented circumstances? Jesus says it does not matter whether the offense was real or not. If we feel antagonism or bitterness or resentment, if we detect even a twinge of vengeance moving in our minds, let it go.

Remember, we are dealing with prayer. Jesus says, "blessed are the peacemakers" (Matt. 5:9). Paul says, "so far as it depends on you, be at peace with all men" (Rom. 12:18). After we pray, there may be actions that need to be taken to promote peace. When we come to pray, the issue is completely in our own hearts.

Finally, the Master says that this forgiveness is to extend to *anyone*. Our hearts tend to put people into different categories and conclude that we can treat them differently. Jesus wipes that out. No matter who the source of the hurt is, we must forgive. They may be the most hateful people on the face of the earth. They may have been the source of multiplied pain for you and the ones you love. They may be completely closed to the idea of reconciliation. They may even be glad that you are experiencing pain because of their actions. Yet, if we are to join the Father in the work of glorifying Jesus Christ, we must deal with all the bitterness in our own souls. Just as the Lord has forgiven us, we must let it go; send it away; clear the record.

For many, forgiveness is not easy to give. But there is no alternative. Christians, who have understood the grace of God in Jesus Christ, forgive. Many years ago, I was visiting in the home of a doctor who oversaw a small hospital in a remote region. At dinner, he received a call from a nurse. She was trying to insert a needle for an IV but had not been able to do so. She wanted the doctor to come and do it for her. He explained that he could not come and that, if she kept on trying, she would succeed. Unconvinced, the nurse said she could not. I will never forget his response. "Then he is going to die, and it will be your fault." He hung up. He saw the look on my face and assured me she would be able to do it when she faced the seriousness of the situation and the reality that there was no other option. Again, I admit, forgiveness is difficult. But there is no alternative.

If we are serious about unlocking the potential for blessing in prayer, we must get serious about forgiveness. Neil Anderson, in *The Bondage Breaker*, summarizes the issues and concerns we have about dealing with the bitterness of unforgiveness.[2] I would strongly urge you to get a copy of that book. Working from what he says, let me make some suggestions to help clear bitterness in the heart.

First, if you have never done this or if you have let things pile up over an extended period, begin by sitting down and making a list of everyone you feel any bitterness towards. Take time with this. Pushing a hurt out of your mind is not the same thing as forgiveness. At times, we subconsciously build a protective layer around hurt. It is still there, but we keep it out of the conscience day by day. These repressed pains are a constant drain on our lives, even though they never come to the surface. Ask the Lord to help you identify every hurt that has never been resolved in forgiveness.

In each case, identify the event which caused the hurt. Name it. Name it in its true nature. It is okay to be honest about the situation since you are not dredging something up for gossip or revenge, but to send it away and to clear the record in forgiveness. Forgive people for particular offenses, not simply because they cause you a vague sense of antagonism.

When you have your list, go down it person by person, event by event. Let them go; send the offense away; forgive. Take it out of your hands and place the responsibility of justice into the capable hands of your Father. Remember that whenever you forgive, you will suffer loss. Stop trying to even the score and determine that the hurt will stop with you. In each case, remember the promise that the Father knows what you need. He is wonderfully able to make up for the loss you have experienced. Forgiveness does not change what happened and it does not change the person you forgive. It does set you free. Bitterness destructively controls your inner being; forgiveness breaks the power of the person over you and sets you free to live in fellowship with your Lord.

Once you have completed the exercise and are confident that you have dealt with everything you can remember, do not do it again. Move forward. Having been released from the chains of the past, live well in the immediate present. Keep short accounts of offenses. Train yourself to take relationships into consideration each time you come to speak with your Father. If we listen to the Lord and forgive each time we come before Him, our lives will be peaceful and our praying vital. "Whenever you stand praying, forgive" (Mark 11:25).

CHAPTER SIX

Humility in Prayer

But the tax collector, standing some distance away,
was even unwilling to lift up his eyes to heaven, but was
beating his breast, saying, 'God, be merciful to me,
the sinner!'
I tell you, this man went to his house justified rather
than the other; for everyone who exalts himself will be
humbled, but he who humbles himself will be exalted.
Luke 18:13-14

As we continue to look at what Jesus has to say about prayer, we move away from the Sermon on the Mount. The first four lessons all pointed to the freedom of approach which God offers in prayer. The final four lessons all deal with the incredible potential of faith-filled prayer. Between these two groups are two lessons on what our hearts must be like in order to enter true fellowship with the Father in prayer. The first is forgiveness. "Whenever you stand praying, forgive, if you have anything against anyone" (Mark 11:25). The second is humble faith. "For everyone who exalts himself will be humbled, and he who humbles himself will be exalted" (Luke 14:11).

The concept of humble faith in prayer is taught in two parables at the beginning of Luke 18. The first story is about a widow. In the Lord's time, this woman was in a particularly vulnerable position. Someone was after her, trying to take advantage of her dilemma. She was desperate for legal protection from the government. That was her only hope. The judge, however, was not the slightest bit interested in her case. She was just not important. Day after day she pestered the judge until, in frustration and fatigue, he ruled in her favor. She succeeded by persevering.

The second story relates an incident in which two very different individuals go into the temple to pray. They both come to the place that the Lord designated to meet with His people. One, a Pharisee, offers a prayer of self-congratulation. The other, a tax collector, faces his terrible need and appeals for God's mercy.

Before we dive into these stories, we must note that humble faith in prayer is not the main point of either one. The first story is about continuing in prayer. The lesson to take away is the necessity and value of persistent prayer. The second story is not so much about prayer as the need for humility before the Lord. Jesus states the main point Himself, "Everyone who exalts himself will be humbled, and he who humbles himself will be exalted" (Luke 14:11). Yet together, they illustrate the need to pray in humble faith.

Before we return to the parables, we should do a short review of some basic theology. No one since the Fall has ever been worthy of a relationship with God. At the beginning, God created mankind (Adam and Eve) with the potential and the opportunity for direct contact and fellowship with Himself. In fact, that relationship was the primary reason for their existence, and for the first couple, the interaction was free and enriching. Sin changed all that. It cancelled the fellowship and permanently altered the makeup of the human race. The plans of the living God are not easily thwarted. In His grace, He immediately began executing a program which would finally restore men and women to His original intention. Sin was the obstacle. Dealing with it required the self-sacrifice of God on the cross in the person of Jesus Christ. In His death, the complete removal of the guilt of sin was made possible. With sin out of the way, the enriching relationship with God was again open to us.

The Old Testament was given to help us understand the message of God in Jesus Christ. The book of Leviticus is particularly important in revealing the value and necessity of sacrifice. The book was given to show the ancient people of God what would be required to have fellowship with Him. The early chapters of that book contain teachings on the various types of sacrifice. They touched every part of Israeli life. The culture is very unfamiliar to most of us, but the teaching of the chapters on sacrifice can be summed up as follows: *the basis of fellowship with God is always and only a sacrifice.* Yet none of the sacrifices of Leviticus were enough. They were only pictures which foreshadowed the perfect work Jesus Christ would accomplish when He gave Himself as the Lamb of God on the cross.

In both the Old and the New Testament, bold offers are made for people to come to God. We have already considered some of those in our study of prayer. In the Sermon on the Mount, Jesus told the crowd that when they prayed, they should get alone with God and He would take note of the prayer. Jesus could only make that offer because of what He would do in giving His own life to open the way to heaven and the heart of God.

A Christian is a person in a living relationship with God Himself. That relationship begins and continues eternally because of the benefit of Jesus' sacrificial work. Paul can say, "for through Him we both [Jews and Gentiles] have our access in one Spirit to the Father" (Eph. 2:18). The writer of Hebrews puts it this way: "Therefore, brethren, since we have confidence to enter the holy place [the presence of God] by the blood of Jesus... let us draw near" (Heb. 10:19, 22).

Since this is true, humility should influence our every

thought as we come to pray. The first time we come to pray, our hope is in what Jesus has done for us. If we complete a lifetime of sacrificial service for the sake of the Lord Jesus Christ, our hope will still be the same. Our service in no way diminishes our need to come in Jesus' name. Faithfulness to God will deepen our love and enrich our experience of the Triune God, but the foundation of our relationship is always His sacrifice on our behalf.

A heart of humility towards God is the main point of the second story from Luke 18. Two men went to pray. They both went to the right place, the place where God said He would meet with men. Both prayed. The difference between the two was the basis of their prayers.

We need to be fair to the Pharisee. These men gave themselves to study and discipline in order to honor God. They believed the Old Testament to be the Word of God and memorized large portions of it. They studied it, meditated on it, and meticulously sought to follow its teaching. When this man said he was not like other men, we should assume that he was accurate. He was not a swindler, or unjust, or an adulterer. He practiced personal discipline (fasting) and financial discipline (tithing). He was in the temple to pray, since prayer was a regular part of his daily routine. How many of us could match his zeal? We have a tendency to attach the word "hypocrite" to the Pharisees as if their lives were a complete sham, but if you saw a real one and watched his life closely, it would be hard not to be impressed. Paul says of his own experience as a Pharisee that no one could find fault with his life when it was compared to the law (Php. 3:5-6). We must not underestimate the achievement of these men, nor the personal cost involved in reaching these heights. The problem with the Pharisee was not that he had aimed high in his attempt to honor God, but that he supposed that his efforts gave him the Lord's acceptance and approval.

According to Jesus, the misconception concerning what he had achieved had two terrible results in the Pharisee. The first was a lack of faith; his confidence before God was in his resumé. The second was his lack of love; he viewed those who could not keep up with contempt. His pride led to a contemptuous statement about the tax collector in which he actually condemned himself: "God, I thank You that I am not... like this tax collector" (Luke 18:11).

Think about the tax collector. He represented the other end of the spiritual spectrum. If you had known him, you would have disliked him. Tax collectors were hated and shunned by respectable society. In the process of collecting taxes, they cheated and betrayed the people of God and constantly broke the law of God. The only motivation for entering the profession was greed. These men collaborated with the ungodly and brutal Roman government to get rich. On that day, as he approached the temple, many worshipers would have inwardly felt the same repulsion the Pharisee expressed.

Regardless of what anyone thought of him, he came and he made an approach to God. He did not come too close. He did not lift his eyes toward heaven in the typical Jewish manner, but he did come. He did not hide his condition from God, nor did he defend himself against the Pharisee's disdain. He was the exact sinner the Pharisee had pointed out and he made no attempt to dodge or to explain or to defend. One thing motivated his prayer: his need. One thing gave him hope: the saving mercy of God. The prayer prevailed. He went home justified, freed from the penalty of his sin.

In the first parable, the dominating feature is the need for humility to be mixed with faith. The widow in the story was by nature humbled. She knew that she was open to all sorts of exploitation in society. The judge was not motivated to act on her behalf. He was not a man of compassion, nor was he concerned about justice. She had nothing with which to win him to her side. Her need is not revealed, but he was her only hope. He had the power to deliver her. We must understand that her appeal was demeaning to her. It was a daily reminder of how hopeless and unimportant she was. In humility and faith, she persisted, and her need was ultimately met. We will consider the story again as we look at the need for persistence, but here we want to make note of her humble faith.

When we come to our Father in prayer, we have great freedom and potential. All our praying must be tempered by the constant realization that all our access and potential was bought for us by a sacrifice. Every approach we make is in Jesus' name and because of our relationship to Him. If we forget that truth, one of two things will happen.

The first is the problem the Pharisee had. He came on the basis of his own achievement. He came trusting in himself. He had moved from a position of faith. This is a danger anyone can fall into, but particularly when we begin to grow in the Lord. At the beginning, we generally do not know anything, nor have we done anything for the Lord. At that point, humility is generally not a problem. As we gain knowledge of the Bible, as we get involved in the work of God in our churches and communities, and as we make financial and time sacrifices for other people, there is a dangerous and subtle tendency to believe that these acts contribute to our relationship with the Lord. We move from an outlook of true faith. We can start to think that these actions make us more acceptable to Him, giving us a special standing with Him.

If that occurs, a second problem creeps into our thought lives. We can subtly begin to think of others with contempt.

Why don't they spend more time in the Word and in prayer? Why don't they do more at the church? Why don't they make the financial and the time sacrifices I make? How could they fall for that sin?

We must never forget that when we first came to God in prayer, we were heard because of the sacrifice of Jesus Christ, and no matter how far we have come in the process of sanctification, we still come by the same sacrifice. Nothing we have done or will ever do will change that arrangement. We need to recognize this in humble faith if we are to grow in the life of prayer.

This pride can take on another form that we must avoid. One of my first counseling opportunities in ministry was with a man who was also in ministry. He had been struggling in his walk with the Lord. Foolishly, I thought that the session would be easy and straightforward. I began to speak to him about common issues we all encounter. I used my Bible. Yet each time I started reading, he would finish the passage, quoting by memory. He acknowledged every principle I covered, generally with the same language I used, since we had been discipled in the same place by the same individuals. After an hour or so, I was getting embarrassed. There was obviously a problem, but I could not pin it down. In a final effort to help, I asked about his prayer life. The mood changed. After a pause, he told me he had not had a meaningful prayer session for some time. When I asked why, we got to the bottom of his problem. Months before, he had been trapped in sin. I don't remember the details, but it was not some terrible action. However, that event had so devastated him that he was embarrassed to come to God. He had confessed the sin, but every time he came to the Father after that, he was overwhelmed with a sense of being unworthy to be with the Father. He continued to work in the ministry, but his prayer life virtually disappeared.

A point which is easy to overlook about the humility of the tax collector is that he came to the temple to pray at all. He knew that in his sinfulness he was not ready for the presence of God. He also believed that the Lord had an answer for that, and he was willing to come and to receive.

The fact is, in ourselves, we are never worthy to come into the presence of the living God. But if we have committed ourselves to Jesus Christ in faith, we come to the Father because of our association with the Lord. This opportunity for fellowship comes at enormous cost to our Father. He paid a terrible price so that His kindness could be justly available to needy men and women. In faith we humble ourselves and come to God, counting on the Lord Jesus to bring us in.

The eternal God is indescribably great. We sum up that greatness in the word "holy". That holiness, in all its dimensions, should always be before us when we come into His presence. Worship and praise are the natural response to His greatness and His grace. Yet, as great and majestic as He is, the writer of Hebrews says that we can approach Him with boldness and confidence (Heb. 10:19). This boldness is not arrogance or flippancy. It is a consciousness that, although we are not fit for that place in our littleness and our sin, Jesus Christ has made a way for us to come in peace.

What about that time when temptation is strong? At times the very experience of temptation can make us cringe before God. Remember, if temptation did not have an appeal in our beings, it would not be temptation at all. For us as children of God, that pull of sin itself can bring a sense of defilement. If that temptation takes its toll on our flesh and moves us to sin, the pain becomes even greater. While our consciences are in pain, the enemy of our souls is there to accuse and badger us.

We must never take sin lightly. The Lord died on a cross to set us free from both the guilt and the power of sin. That will only take place as we stay close to the Lord. We cannot do this on our own. Paul said that in his flesh lived nothing good (Rom. 7:18). Jesus said to His disciples that they must abide in Him because, apart from Him, they could do nothing (John 15:5). All hope of ever doing the Father's work on this earth depends on staying close to Him in faith. Therefore, no matter what our condition, it is time to go to the Lord for salvation in humble faith.

My own advice is that when the enemy tells you that you are unworthy to come, meet the accusation with a hearty "amen". Then, thank your Father for the costly provision of righteousness that was worked out in the sacrifice of Jesus Christ. Next, move into His presence and allow Him to do what is needful to make salvation real in the area of your need.

One type of pride, which disqualifies us from vital fellowship with God, is trusting in our own goodness. Another type of pride is refusing to come to the Father until we have somehow cleansed ourselves. The right way to pray is in humble faith, approaching the Father fully aware of our need, but, like the tax collector, counting on His grace and kindness for full deliverance.

Section Three:

Potential of Prayer

CHAPTER SEVEN

Keep on Asking

For everyone who asks, receives; and he who seeks,
finds;
and to him who knocks, it will be opened.
Luke 11:10

We turn now to the final group of lessons in our consideration of the Lord's teaching on prayer. The principles we have considered to this point were in two groups. First, there were four general lessons on the great *privilege* in prayer found in the Sermon on the Mount. The essence of prayer is to direct our hearts and our words to God. Second, when we speak, we should use meaningful language, the honest language of our hearts. Third, the relationship of a child to his father should dominate our outlook as we pray. Finally, true and effective prayer focuses on the purposes of the Father on this earth. We are to seek first the kingdom of God in our prayers.

Following these general principles, Jesus turned to the *preparation* for prayer. There we had teaching that focused on two heart issues. Both concern attitudes that we must maintain if we are to join the Father in His work on this earth. The first is a forgiving spirit; the second, true humility.

Four more lessons remain. All of them focus on the *potential* of prayer as we use it in the work God has given us to do. It is the Father's family business. We do not initiate it. We simply join the Lord in what He is doing. We do not do it alone but as part of a band of the children of God known as the church.

In one sense, we could say that the family business is done by three means: the ministry of the Word, the testimony of the saints, and prayer. Two are out front. People must hear the Word of God. We must go and spread that message. Further, people must know of how that message has changed our lives. This could come either in the form of a spoken testimony of how the Lord has met us or by the life testimony of how we have been changed in our conduct. However, if the kingdom of God is to come in people around us, we must also pray. The open ministry of the Word and the secret ministry of prayer must combine for lives to be changed. It is very much like epoxy glue. The glue comes packaged in two parts: the epoxy itself and a hardener. Neither is of any value by itself. Mixed, they form an adhesive of incredible strength. I am afraid that we sometimes lose sight of the fact that the visible ministry by itself is not enough. As important as prayer is, the work cannot be done by prayer alone. However, when those two ministries combine, stunning changes take place in real lives.

Our studies now move to the Lord's teaching on the use of prayer in the family business of building the kingdom of God. Each lesson focuses on the confidence that we should have as we make our requests to the Father.

Jesus takes us first to the need for persistence in prayer. Three important passages relate to this subject. The first is found early in the Lord's ministry as He delivers the Sermon on the Mount (Matt. 7:7-11). The other two are in the book of Luke (11:5-13; 18:1-8).

The Matthew 7 passage has a broader application than just prayer. It describes the entire expression of the heart of a person who is seeking first the kingdom of God. Its application to prayer becomes clear when Jesus uses almost exactly the same words to teach His disciples to pray in Luke 11.

We considered the scene earlier. A group of unnamed disciples asks Jesus to teach them to pray (Luke 11:1). Jesus is ready and more than willing to give them instruction. The order of the instruction is critical to His teaching on persistence.

Jesus begins where He did early in His ministry at the Sermon on the Mount. He starts with an abbreviated version of the Lord's Prayer. He tells them that when they pray, they are to shape their requests around this standard: seek first the kingdom of God. Then they are to ask the Father to supply what is needed as they live for His glory.

He then moves on to a parable (Luke 11:5-8). As we look at this story, we must make a careful differentiation between an allegory and a parable. In an allegory, every detail of the story has a point and teaches something. In a parable, the story is told to make one point. Our attention should be concentrated on that point. The rest of the details of the story are just necessary to make the story work. The point of this parable is the reward of persistence in prayer.

The story begins with a man caught in a socially embarrassing situation. Everyone in that culture was expected to be prepared for guests. This did not require elaborate provisions, since most people would not have the financial resources for that kind of preparedness. It simply required that a small amount be set aside for an unexpected visitor. This man had been caught unprepared. His sense of shame compelled him to go to a friend and beg for help. It seems like such a simple request. What was the big deal about getting up and handing the man a few loaves of bread? He had the bread, so what was the holdup? Yet, it was not at all simple. People lived in one room houses. Nighttime brought with it real dangers. Getting ready for bed involved a process of locking oneself into the house and often barricading the door. Then everyone found their place on the floor and went to sleep. To open the door, the entire family would have to get up while the unlocking procedure was carried out. After handing over the requested loaves, the door would need to be relocked, the barricade replaced, and the family resettled. It was not impossible, but it was inconvenient. The whole process would be made worse by the thought that the situation was avoidable. His friend should not have let this happen.

Therefore, his friend said no. He was not willing to go through the inconvenience. But the man in need was undeterred. He continued to knock and knock and knock until the household's sleep was finally disrupted and the request was met. The success was not related to friendship. He got what he wanted because he refused to be denied. That is the sole point of the story. Jesus is not teaching about the character of God. Later, in this passage, the Lord will address the nature of the Father. Here, He teaches His disciples not to give up easily in prayer.

The Lord then begins to apply the parable to the disciples using words that are almost exactly what He said in Matthew 7:7. "So I say to you, ask, and it will be given to you; seek, and you will find; knock, and it will be opened to you" (Luke 11:9). Each of the verbs, "ask," "seek," and "knock", indicates ongoing action. The verse could be expressed, "Ask and keep on asking; seek and keep on seeking; knock and keep on knocking." To encourage this kind of tenacity, Jesus gives a promise. "For everyone who asks [and keeps on asking], receives; and he who seeks [and keeps on seeking], finds; and to him who knocks [and keeps on knocking], it will be opened" (Luke 11:10). The key word here is "everyone". There are no exceptions.

A reminder is necessary at this point. There are those that use this passage to endorse the idea that God is waiting to make you rich or happy or successful if only you keep on asking Him. It is a very popular teaching. But that totally misses what the Lord is saying.

Jesus had just returned from His time with His Father. The disciples did not ask how to get things from God. They wanted to know how to pray. Jesus first gives direction to their praying by taking them back to what He already taught concerning seeking first the kingdom of God. They are to persevere in those prayers. The motivation for praying should be the Father's business. The kingdom of God, not our own kingdom, is at stake in the prayer.

Listen to the Lord again as He underlines what He said. "For everyone who asks, receives; and he who seeks, finds; and to him who knocks, it will be opened" (Luke 11:10). Again, the key word in the whole verse is "everyone". Regardless of who they are, everyone who keeps on asking receives. Put yourself in that "everyone". I have been greatly helped and inspired in my walk with the Lord by the biographies of the great saints in church history. The lives of these men and women of faith give us testimonies, and testimony is one of the tools God uses in building His church. There is a downside, however, to all this which must be avoided. We can look at men like Hudson Taylor in much the same way as we look at great athletes. We can admire them while backing off from trying to imitate them. Great athletes possess natural abilities that we do not; we live in separate worlds. No amount of inspiration or training can make a slow runner fast. Most of us are genetically limited in that realm. When we come to pray, it is a different story. Prayer is the experience of needy people coming in faith to an all-sufficient God. It does not require some spiritual "gene". We qualify because of our need. There is hope because of the vast, all-encompassing salvation which the Father has made available in Jesus Christ. We all fit in the "everyone" category. The only requirement Jesus puts upon us is persistence. Real prayer involves an intensity of desire which keeps on coming to a loving Father until the answer is realized.

In what sense then should we understand "keep on asking"? Think again about the parable. The man had one very clear and specific request. He needed bread to avoid dishonoring a visitor. He had a friend who could supply that need. He kept on asking until the need was met. Jesus is not talking about a consistent prayer life, as important as that is. He is speaking about coming to God about a need and holding that request before Him until He moves.

As we go on in the passage, the Lord turns the subject to the heart of God. He is not like the sleeping friend of the parable. In order to underline this truth, He appeals to the natural affection of a father for his son (Luke 11:11-13). A good father would not ignore the genuine need of his son or daughter. He gives hungry children the food they need. He does not play sadistic games with them; he does not give them harmful or useless things when they ask for food. Unlike us at our very best, our heavenly Father is supremely good. He is never thoughtless, distracted, or abusive. The instinctive desire to take care of our own is placed in us by the One who is never tarnished in His heart by evil thoughts. His love is consistent. Seek Him honestly and persistently, and you will be blessed.

Jesus finishes His teaching on an unexpected note. "How much more will your heavenly Father give the Holy Spirit to those who ask Him?" (Luke 11:13). Jesus started with the Lord's Prayer, which has seeking His kingdom as its aim. What we need most in carrying out that goal is the work of the Spirit of God in our lives and in the lives of others. In a sense, all the other petitions that are consistent with the opening lines of the prayer lead to the need for the provision of the Spirit. There is no doubt that the Father will give the Spirit of God to everyone who asks.

Before we move to apply this passage, we should touch again briefly on the story Jesus gives in Luke 18. The parable has many of the same elements we find in Luke 11. Let me remind you of what we saw in Chapter 6. A woman is in great need, but, unlike the friend of the first story, the need is not because of her own negligence. She is a widow, and widows were in a particularly vulnerable situation in that culture. Someone is oppressing her, and the only hope of relief is in the action of a judge who is neither compassionate nor just. She is totally unimportant, so he is not motivated to help. He refuses her request. There is no other option; if he does not rule on her behalf, she is finished. She makes herself a pest; she does not go away, and she does not stay quiet. Finally, the exasperated judge relents and gives her the help she needs. Again, the teaching is not about God. He is not like the selfish and heartless judge. The focus is on the woman, and the point is this: never give up in prayer.

Jesus relates this story to teach us to keep praying and not to faint, or to give up, or to become disheartened. The parable is connected closely to the difficulties that will surround the last days before the Lord returns. It could get tough for God's people. In those days, as in any other day, our hope is in God. He is our Father. He is for us. No matter what He allows, we must keep on praying. He hears our cry and at the right time, the blessing will come. We can count on His steadfast love.

These parables address two dangers that face us in our praying. The first is superficiality. Prayer is not a formality or a spiritual routine to be kept up. It is a vital part of the powerful work of God to bring the delivering and renewing benefits of Jesus' work on the cross to bear in the lives of needy people. Yet, when we get together in prayer times, we so often do not detect that vitality. We are often very casual about what we are going to ask God. We take prayer requests. We pray. We come back in a week, and we cannot remember our prayers.

We should ask ourselves after a prayer time, "If the Father granted every request, what eternal benefit would there be? Would our prayers make a significant difference in anyone's life?"

In prayer, we bow before the Lord of the universe. The Father, who gave His Son in the sacrifice of the cross, is totally committed to seeing His plan for salvation completed. Jesus Christ is relentlessly working to build the church through both the evangelism of those who do not know Him and the sanctification of those who do.

The Spirit of God is passionate about Jesus Christ being glorified before real people who are alive right now. When we come to God, we do not need to bring the energy. All we need to do is to allow the living God to share His life and His energy with us. He is never half-hearted. He is the Lord of glory, God all-wise and almighty. He knows exactly what needs to be done to bless men and exactly how that can be best accomplished. We do not need to bring the wisdom. We simply need to look around and allow Him to inspire our hearts. He brings unlimited resources to the table to bring His will to pass. We do not need to bring the resources. We simply need to tap into His limitless supply. He is all in, and if we want to join Him, we are also going to have to be all in.

Second, the parables address the problem of discouragement. Jesus says to keep on praying. No matter how tough the fight in prayer or how long the wait, we should not lose heart. Everything in the kingdom of God depends on His intervention. We must grab hold of Him and not let go until He acts.

Listen to the way the Lord puts it. "Now He was telling them a parable to show that at all times they ought to pray and not to lose heart" (Luke 18:1). He admonishes them that they should pray "at all times." No adversity they would ever face should stop their praying. It says they "ought" to pray. The meaning is a bit stronger than that. It is *necessary*. It is not only something they should do to fulfill their duty, there is a *must* to it. In the time immediately preceding Christ's return, the pressures of living for God will be so intense that a persevering prayer life will be necessary if they are to be faithful. There is no alternative either for them or for us. Either we keep praying or we will keep losing heart. One or the other will be true. The idea of losing heart implies a failure of courage. It is a failure of character. It means to quit because of cowardice. The Lord says that persevering prayer results in the strength of character to not only keep on praying but to keep on living for Him in a world controlled by fallen men.

Paul uses this same word, "to lose heart", several times. He says that, because of the certainty of the power of the gospel, despite all the opposition to preaching, he does not lose heart (2 Cor. 4:1). He tells the Ephesians that, even though his imprisonment continues, it is all part of the plan of God (Eph. 3:13). He wanted the believers to know that so they would not lose heart. Again, recognizing that doing good for others does not always lead to kind treatment, he encourages the church to not grow weary in doing good (2 Thess. 3:13). Do not give up despite the difficulty. In time, God will honor selfless service.

Jesus was preparing His disciples for the difficult road

ahead as they established the church on the earth. He says a tenacious prayer experience will strengthen them with the necessary fortitude (moral courage) to keep on going.

As in the parable of the friend's search for bread, the widow in the story had a specific and well-defined need. She also had a clear understanding of who could meet that need. She refused to change her request or to go to some other source. In the end, she was rewarded for her tenacity. If we pray, we also will be strengthened for life in this age and find that our cries to the Father are finally effective. We must ask and keep on asking.

As we listen to the words of the Lord, a question often haunts us. Why are answers to prayers delayed? Why do we need to keep on praying? The Father is quite capable of giving us what we ask immediately. Why does He delay?

The Bible does not answer that question directly. Maybe that is because there is no single reason. There are hints, but there is no place we can go and find His reasons explained. Because of that, I venture out with great caution. I will give a few possible explanations. You are free to disagree with them. They all come from verses and passages that are speaking of other things and, therefore, the conclusions must be held lightly.

Before we go to any of those passages, we need to be clear about what is not the issue. To those who do not know God, yet pray, He often seems distant and uncaring. However, "your Father knows what you need before you ask Him" (Matt. 6:8). Our Father is vitally involved in the events of this life. When we join His work as we pray, He is one hundred percent behind us. There is no lack of capacity or desire on His part. Our lives are encased in a love from which nothing can separate us. No matter how confusing things become in our lives, and particularly in our praying, we must never move from that confidence.

Why does the Father delay? A first explanation could come from the parable of the widow. We saw there that Jesus says that there are two alternatives in our lives; either we keep praying or we will keep losing heart. We pray about things that are important to us, both in the promotion of His kingdom and in living our daily lives. We are more likely to continue praying while we wait for the answer. While we are in the presence of the Father, seeking His answer in prayer and in the Word, we are strengthened. The interaction with God in calling to Him for an answer in one area of life gives Him the opportunity to strengthen us for courageous living in every area of life. He may delay simply to keep us close for our own sake. Then, as the parable says, the answer will come.

A second possible explanation is the limitation of our own understanding. We pray for an intervention of God in some individual or circumstance. Meanwhile, the Lord of the harvest is watching over a very grand project. He is building the church worldwide. I do not believe any of us, no matter how hard we try, can grasp the breadth of the work of God at any given moment. We often get something of the Elijah syndrome, "I have been very zealous for the LORD, the God of hosts... And I alone am left" (1 Kings 19:14). Somehow Elijah, a man who served God faithfully, had missed that there were still more than seven thousand worshipers in Israel who were loyal to the true God at that terrible time in their history. Elijah had the up-front ministry, and God was at work in him. But hidden from sight, He was also working in many others. Although they would not share the ministry, they were there, faithfully standing for the Lord behind the scenes.

The Father wants to answer our prayers. But the answers

must fit into a greater plan. I wonder how much delay is simply due to the Lord's timing. There is something happening in lives around us that we would not believe if we were told (Hab. 1:5). In the meantime, we are not to become passive but we are to keep on intently seeking and asking the Father to work. Then, when the answer comes, we will be able to grasp the greatness and the breadth of the Spirit's work in a fuller way.

Finally, I would suggest that the seeming delays at times have something to do with the unseen spiritual conflict that rages around us. When Paul describes the ministry of the church in the book of Ephesians, he gets to the matter of prayer in the final chapter as part of the section on spiritual conflict (Eph. 6:11-20). He likens the work of the kingdom of God to a wrestling match. It would be hard to find a picture which more forcefully combines intensity and closeness. Every day, we engage in a fight. The enemy is not in some distant land. He is as near as the opponent in a wrestling match. Further, Paul says we must put on spiritual armor, go out, and confront spiritual darkness just as a Roman soldier went out to fight a visible enemy. It is hand to hand, face to face. He says we have two great weapons in that conflict: the Word of God and prayer. Be clear, we pray *to* God, not *against* the devil. Yet, if the power of Jesus Christ's death and resurrection life is going to be experienced where the Father has placed us, we will have to pray. There is strong indication that we must keep on praying because of that conflict. We must hold out in faith before the Father until our enemy backs off. We are to support each other and to have one another's back. Possibly the answers are delayed to keep us alert and faithful in prayer on behalf of others.

Vital prayer is persevering prayer; we must keep on asking. Effective prayer is also persevering; everyone who keeps on asking will receive.

CHAPTER EIGHT

Have Faith in God

*And Jesus answered saying to them, "Have faith
in God. Truly I say to you, whoever says to this
mountain, 'Be taken up and cast into the sea,' and
does not doubt in his heart, but believes that what
he says is going to happen, it will be granted him.
Therefore I say to you, all things for which you pray
and ask, believe that you have received them, and they
will be granted you."*
Mark 11:22-24

The just live by faith. That lesson is taught from the beginning to the end of the Bible. It is true that faith is the
means to entering into a blessed relationship with God, but
that is not the end. According to Hebrews 11, the just continue to live out their lives with an outlook of faith. What is
faith anyway? How does it relate to prayer?

The passage before us relates to an event which we already looked at in Chapter 5. In the final week of His ministry, Jesus came to Jerusalem for the last time. Because of
Passover, the city of Jerusalem was flooded with visitors.
Jesus and His disciples were staying outside the city, probably with Mary and Martha in Bethany. On a trip into the city
early in the week, Jesus saw a lone fig tree along the road.
He was hungry, and he looked for some fruit. Finding none,
He cursed the tree and it withered. So often, when we look
at the story, we ask why He did that. The disciples however
were not concerned about the "why" of the action but were

101

dumbfounded by the fact that the tree immediately shriveled at His word.

Peter expressed the group's ongoing amazement when they passed the tree again. It had not simply wilted; it was dead from the roots up. The disciples were once again confronted with the Lord's complete command of nature.

Jesus is not content to use this event simply as evidence of His own power. He takes advantage of the situation as a teaching moment. Within two months, this unlikely band of followers will be in charge of building the church of Jesus Christ. He will not be visibly with them. They will need faith and courage to act in His name. And so, He speaks to them about the authority and the power that will be in their hands.

Have faith in God. Trust and rely upon the Father just as I have relied upon Him. Do not look at this event as a demonstration of My power but as evidence of the way the Father will act on your behalf as you work in the kingdom.

Before we move forward to the relationship of faith and prayer, we need to remind ourselves of the nature of biblical faith. The secular world has embraced the idea of the power of faith and twisted its meaning. We see it in the entertainment world. How many stories present a character faced with seemingly impossible odds? The character is then told that no matter how difficult things look, something will happen if only he will believe. The hapless team will win, or Santa's sleigh will fly, or whatever. In the picture, faith is a force that causes things to happen.

We find the same thing when we move this concept from entertainment to self-help. Visualize what you want to be in five years. Picture yourself in that condition. Put the goal on a piece of paper and hang it on your mirror. Tell yourself that is who you really are. Go for your goal and the dream will become reality if you maintain your faith. Again, confidence in your dream, or belief in yourself, is seen as a force which makes it happen. If you can believe, you can have it. Your hope is in the strength of your faith.

Sadly, some have moved this thinking into the Christian world. I remember listening years ago to a radio evangelist who told his hearers that he drove a Mercedes because he had "Mercedes faith". They drove Fords because they had "Ford faith". If they strengthened their faith, they too could drive a luxury vehicle.

Biblical faith is quite different. First is the fact that true faith is all about God and not faith. The value of faith is not in how much you have, but where you place that faith.

My first plane ride occurred on my way home from college. It was a short jump from Tallahassee, Florida to Orlando, Florida. The late afternoon skies were filled with thunderstorms. Yet, despite the weather conditions, I had enough confidence in the plane and the pilots to board. Once airborne, my confidence was shaken. We bumped our way to central Florida through a dark canyon between massive storm cloud formations. Lightning flashed continually. My hands gripped the arm rests. Each time the plane seemed to sink in the air, I pulled up. I had studied enough physics to realize the foolishness of my efforts. I exercised faith getting on the plane. The success of the trip to Orlando was the result of the plane and the pilots I trusted. The power of that plane and the skill of the pilots was not dependent on my faith. All I did was commit myself to them. They did the rest, bringing me safely to Orlando.

I think again of the days when we were building the school where I work. The first dormitory was a block and concrete structure. We built support walls of reinforced block. The decking for each floor arrived in massive pre-stressed concrete slabs. No one was capable of lifting them into place. The crane that was brought to set the slabs in place was incredibly powerful. After attaching the concrete to the boom, the operator simply moved a lever forward, and up they went. Without the operator, nothing would have happened, but no one would credit the person in the cab with moving the slabs. They did not move because the operator's arms were powerful. A very small person could have done it. The operator could have been weak with sickness and still have finished the work. All he did was use the mechanisms that activated his very powerful tool.

That is why Jesus, speaking to that band of insignificant men, said, "Have faith in God" (Mark 11:22). Move your entire confidence to God. Get it there. Leave it there. Trust Him to act on your behalf. He is ready and willing to do so.

Having faith in God necessitates that we get in line with the Father's purpose. We need to back up here and think about why Jesus cursed the fig tree. This was not an outburst of anger because Jesus' own hunger had not been satisfied. This was a symbolic act, a picture parable. The fig tree was used in the Old Testament as a picture of Israel. God had a purpose for that group of people. Jesus had come first to Israel to call them back to God.

For the most part, the Lord of glory was rejected. Before the week was over, the leaders of that nation would renounce any relationship to Jesus and have Him executed. When that happened, the special role of Israel would come to an end. They rejected God's purpose for them. The fig tree became an illustration. The Lord spoke, and the Father backed up His words because Jesus was carrying out the purpose of God.

As we just noted, this band of disciples was being prepared to receive an incredible responsibility: "Go therefore and make disciples of all the nations" (Matt. 28:19). They were not being sent out to accumulate wealth so that they and their families could enjoy life. They were being sent out to join the Spirit of God in His great work to glorify Jesus Christ. In the course of that work, they would face challenges which might seem insurmountable. Jesus' encouragement was simple: "Have faith in God" (Mark 11:22). Do not just hope for the best or try to be confident in the face of difficulties. Count on God to work on your behalf as you go forward.

Jesus' first application of having faith is not technically about prayer. He borrows a common idiom from the spiritual teaching of His day about dealing with difficulties. Challenges are pictured as mountains to be moved out of the way. Jesus says that if we speak to them in faith, they will move. In Luke 17:5-6, He uses similar language about speaking to a tree and having it become uprooted and driven away. Again, I would say this is not technically prayer. In prayer we speak to God. Here we exercise authority in the situation as it confronts us. And since we are concerned with prayer in this study, let's go on to the Lord's second application.

"Therefore I say to you, all things for which you pray and ask, believe that you have received them, and they will be granted you" (Mark 11:24). This is the degree to which the Father is ready to back up the efforts of those committed to bringing His will to pass on the earth. Therefore, when we ask the Father to act on this earth for His glory or to supply what is needed to bring that to pass, we should have no doubt about His involvement. We must count on it immediately and hold on as long as necessary. In the Father's time, the right time, it will be given. As children of God and His ser-

105

vants on this earth, we should be seeing continual evidence of His working in our realm of influence.

What is required in prayer is not great faith but well-placed faith. As they watched the Lord, the disciples must have concluded His faith explained a lot about the success of His ministry. They made a simple, direct request of the Lord: "Increase our faith!" (Luke 17:5). His response was just as direct. "If you had faith like a mustard seed, you would say to this mulberry tree, 'Be uprooted and be planted in the sea'; and it would obey you" (Luke 17:6). His answer was simple. They did not need more faith. They needed to act on the faith they had. There is no doubt that the strength of our faith can grow as we see the truth of God's Word work out in our lives. Yet, the key to success is never the strength of the faith we exercise but the greatness of the One we trust. In prayer, we are asked to place our confidence in the strength and wisdom of God and in His faithfulness to act on our behalf.

Another important connection exists between faith and prayer. Faith is a necessary element of prayer, but prayer is also a necessary element in developing and maintaining a heart of faith. In the last chapter, we looked at the parable of the widow in Luke 18. Luke tells us that the purpose of that parable is to teach that we ought (because it is necessary) always to pray. The reason, he says, is to avoid losing heart, to avoid giving up when things get difficult. The act of prayer enables men to maintain faith even under the extreme pressures of life. That parable, however, is not the only place this truth comes up. The relationship between prayer and faith is also demonstrated in Jesus' healing of a demonized boy.

> When they came to the crowd, a man came up to Jesus, falling on his knees before Him and say-

ing, "Lord, have mercy on my son, for he is a lunatic and is very ill; for he often falls into the fire and often into the water. I brought him to Your disciples, and they could not cure him." And Jesus answered and said, "You unbelieving and perverted generation, how long shall I be with you? How long shall I put up with you? Bring him here to Me." And Jesus rebuked him, and the demon came out of him, and the boy was cured at once (Matt. 17:14-18).

The moment was extremely embarrassing. Jesus had taken Peter, James, and John and gone up a high mountain. While the disciples awaited their return, a desperate father brought a demonized son to them. They had dealt with demons successfully before, but something was different this time. Their commands that the demon leave were met with resistance. As they struggled, a crowd gathered. There was no escape. In their continued failure, they made fools of themselves. The Lord returned and stepped in to deal with the problem. After things calmed down and the disciples were alone with the Lord, the obvious questions were asked. "What happened? We have dealt with demons before. Why were we not able to cast it out? What went wrong this time?"

To get the full picture of how the Lord responded, we must combine His words recorded in Matthew with those in Mark's account. First, in Matthew, He uses words similar to what we have seen in previous passages. "Because of the littleness of your faith" (Matt. 17:20). The work of God is a work of faith, and, at that moment, their faith was not sufficient for the demands of the situation. Then comes a stinging word. "If you have faith the size of a mustard seed..." If you just had a tiny amount of faith, you could move mountains. Yet then, as if anticipating that they will improve in the future, He adds, "and nothing will be impossible to you."

What can be done to ensure our faith is ready for the serious, unexpected demands of ministry? If we look at the account in Mark, I think we will find an answer. There, Jesus says that this kind of demon "cannot come out by anything but prayer" (Mark 9:29). It is obvious as we look at the passages that both parts of the explanation for their failure fit together. The disciples lacked faith. Prayer was an answer to the situation. Faith is necessary in prayer. But prayer is also a means to increasing faith. In the act of genuine prayer, our focus is on God Himself. We concentrate on the greatness of His person and the certainty of His plan and purpose. Faith is the natural result of understanding who God is, as the object of our faith, and what He is doing on earth.

The principles we have considered in the last two chapters go hand in hand. As we think about both of them, we need to stop and make some practical applications. How can these principles become part of our prayer pattern?

I spoke earlier in the book about my early days of learning to pray. I tried to develop stamina in prayer by forcing myself to remain in prayer for a certain length of time. My problem? I ran out of material. I ran out because I had a very poor understanding of the Christian life and of my place as a tool in God's hands. The God we serve is a Being with a plan. You cannot read the Bible and miss that. He is also a Person of activity. He is always working on this earth. At times, we think that nothing is happening in the spiritual realm. If we could join the Father for a moment in heaven and look out on the vast population of the earth, we would be shocked at the breadth and depth of His work.

When we were born again by the Spirit of God, we were placed into Jesus Christ. He is now our life. He is alive in us to complete what He started in His incarnation. We become part of His body to accomplish His purpose. If we could look at the work God is doing from heaven's vantage point, we would see that He is doing that work through His people. On the day of Pentecost, the Father added three thousand people to the fledgling body of Christ. It was His work. Peter preached. Peter had the awesome privilege of joining with the Father in His work. Paul preached in Philippi, and the Spirit of God worked through him to begin building a church in that city. He met with opposition and was ultimately beaten and thrown in prison, but his ministry went on. God was doing a work to prepare the jailor of the prison to hear the gospel. Paul sang praises to God in his pain, and the Lord created circumstances to enable Paul to lead the jailor to Jesus Christ. Through that beating and imprisonment, Paul was allowed to join the Father in the family business of seeking to save the lost.

This is not only true for the apostles in the New Testament times; it is true for every member of the body of Christ. If we have Jesus as our life, our Father is working in our circumstances to give us the honor of participating in His work. Knowing that we have a part motivates us to action. Knowing that the bulk of the work is in His hands keeps us in peace.

How should these facts shape our prayer lives? First, it tells us that the material to pray about is right around us. It is in what is often called our "sphere of influence". It is happening in the immediate present. Our praying is part of our living. It is part of how we bring the purpose of God to bear on this earth. It is wonderful to pray for people in distant lands, and I would not want to discourage that in any way. As we grow in Christ, our capacity to enter into vital prayer for them increases. However, these people often are too generic. We perceive them as people without faces and, more importantly, without serious flaws. Therefore, our requests to God tend to become generic, broad, and lacking in real trust.

As you begin to think about what you should pray for, begin with the people right around you and their present needs. This would include our families, neighbors, fellow students, coworkers, members of our churches, and all the people we meet casually but regularly in our daily routines. We must each ask ourselves, "Where is God working around me?" Jesus did not meet the needs of everyone who passed Him, but He was always alert to the hearts his Father had prepared. Ask the Lord to show you what opportunities He is creating. He is doing this; lift your eyes and look for it.

These will be real people with real faces with whom you have real history. They have opinions and sinful bents, and they are not always as ready to hear the words of life like the unknown people who wait for the gospel in distant places. Being involved with them in prayer will require all the faith, humility, forgiveness, and tenacity that the Lord has told us about in His previous words.

How can we pray for these people? I learned a great lesson in prayer from a very effective missionary leader. His prayer responsibilities were enormous. As field director, he was responsible for a whole group of missionaries. He had his own church planting work to think about. There was also his family. We could add more, but you get the picture. How could he pray for such a vast number of people? Here is what I learned.

He prayed *thoughtfully*. He prepared to pray. I find that some people have a problem here. There is a belief that in prayer we must just follow the lead of the Spirit, and pray what comes. We certainly need the enablement of the Spirit to pray, but that does not mean we cannot think. I am a Bible teacher. I have studied the Bible and read about it for over 40 years. In this small book, I am thinking about what the Lord Himself says about prayer. As I write the chapters, I have spent a lot of time organizing material, thinking about where people struggle in prayer, and how I can best bring the truth of the Word to them so they can launch out into the deep in prayer. That means taking time to ask myself exactly what it is that I want to say. When we sit in church, we hope that the pastor will be filled with the Spirit as he speaks. Simultaneously, we also hope that he has done the hard work of preparation so that he speaks with the power of clarity. The same should be true in our praying. We need to think. What are the real needs we see in the realm of our influence? What does the Lord indicate in His Word He is able to do about those needs? The missionary leader was first observant and thoughtful about the situation and people around him.

Second, he was *concise*. He worked out his request for each situation into a single sentence. When a man gets ready to preach, he should be able to state what he is going to say in a single sentence. If not, he is probably not clear about what he wants to say. If he is not clear, the chances that the congregation will understand clearly are not very high. But concise prayers demand faith.

The Bible contains a story of Bartimaeus (Mark 10:46-52). He was blind and cried out for mercy from the Lord. Jesus asked that he be brought to Him. Then He asked him a somewhat strange question, "What do you want me to do for you?" (Mark 10:51). The man was blind. Was that not obvious? But the Lord did not let him off on this. The man had to state his need specifically. In doing so, he had to face what he was trusting God to do. Jesus could have had mercy on Bartimaeus in many ways. He was collecting alms. The Lord could have given him a big gift. Jesus could have made him part of His team. "Have mercy on me" is a generic prayer.

111

We tend to like to leave it there. Jesus did not. He forced the blind man to commit himself in faith right in front of everyone. How many people at that point in time had been healed of blindness by a religious teacher? If Jesus said He could not heal him, Bartimaeus would be humiliated once again. But the Lord loves to be trusted and was delighted to meet the request.

This is more than a technique. It seems to me that we find a lot of biblical warrant for it. The recorded prayers of the Bible are short and pointed. Think of Jesus the night before the crucifixion. He speaks to Peter about the whole group. He tells Peter that Satan had obtained permission to sift the disciples like wheat. The men Jesus trained for the building of the church were going to go through sifting that night. To encourage them, the Lord says, "But I have prayed for you" (Luke 22:32). That alone would be encouraging, yet He goes further, "But I have prayed for you, that your faith may not fail." A lot would happen that night, things about which prayer could be offered, but Jesus recognized the key concern in the conflict was that the trials would not cause their faith in Him to collapse. And of course, He was heard. Look again at Acts 4. The disciples had assessed the threats of the religious leaders. They had faced how those threats would collide with the clear direction from the Lord to be witnesses. Their prayer was simple, "And now, Lord, take note of their threats, and grant that Your bond-servants may speak Your word with all confidence" (Acts 4:29). That is where they were and that is what they needed from their Father. They were powerfully met.

Then consider the prayers of Paul, particularly in Ephesians, Colossians, and Philippians. Paul had the oversight of all the Gentile churches. He tells us that in his prayer life, he prayed for them continually. These letters contain some of the prayers he was offering for them. Think about the prayer for the Philippians (Php. 1:9-11). There was interpersonal conflict in the church. A great deal of the letter gives teaching related to that subject. But Paul does not leave them with teaching alone. He prayed, not simply for their blessing, but that their love might abound more and more. He was specifically asking God to strengthen them so this problem could be resolved.

The missionary of whom I spoke took time before the Lord to think about the circumstances confronting him. After careful thought, he wrote out a prayer and added it to a systematic prayer list.

That leads to our final point. He prayed with *perseverance*. So often, we are not aware if God answers our prayers simply because we do not remember what we asked. That was not so for this man. He prayed repeatedly for each request until he either saw the answer or had deeper insight which enabled him to reshape his prayer. He was praying for things that mattered. He expected the Lord to answer. If that answer came in a short period of time, as it sometimes does, he moved on. If the answer was delayed, he kept on asking. He saw amazing answers to prayer, not because he was a great man of faith, although I am sure he was, but because he saw what was happening where God had placed him. He looked for opportunities in his realm of influence where he could join the Father in His great work.

The wonderful part of writing down concise prayers is that they are easy to remember. The process of thinking out our prayers tends to fix them in our minds so we can remind the Lord of what we are expecting in only a few seconds. Every time we see a person or are reminded of a situation, we can bring it again before the throne of grace.

The Father is anxious to answer prayer. The problem in prayer is never on His side. No matter who we are, if we know Him, He is inviting us to join Him in His work that is going on right around us. If we lift our eyes, consider the need, and appeal to the God of grace with faith and perseverance, we will know the joy of seeing His work fulfilled.

CHAPTER NINE

If Two Agree

*Again I say to you, that if two of you agree on earth
about anything that they may ask,
it shall be done for them by My Father who is
in heaven.
For where two or three have gathered together in My
name, I am there in their midst.*
Matthew 18:19-20

God loves unity. Not that coerced kind of unity where a group is pressured either by force or intimidation to submit to a higher will. Not the kind of unity of uniformity where everyone adopts identical patterns of life and speech. The unity He seeks is the unity of love that develops when different personalities selflessly pull together to achieve a common goal. He loves that kind of unity because it reflects so much of the essential glory of God Himself.

The one eternal God is a Trinity of persons. That has been eternally true. We stumble as we try to grasp that fact. He is holy, completely different. The biblical record is given to help us grasp the nature of the holy God. The more we study the Word, the more we realize that concepts such as omnipresence, omniscience, sovereignty, infinity, (and we could go on), are easier to affirm than to understand. It is the same when we come to the concept of the Trinity. Stating the facts of the Bible can be done in a few sentences. We can create brief statements of faith without much difficulty, but when we attempt to picture or grasp the Trinity, we fail. God is not exactly like anything in our experience. We give illustrations from nature, but they all miss the mark and tend to confuse more than clarify. Although in one sense we cannot comprehend the reality of the Trinity, this truth goes a long way in helping us to understand true godliness.

In his *Systematic Theology,* Wayne Grudem defines the doctrine of the Trinity as follows: "God eternally exists as three persons, Father, Son and Holy Spirit, and each person is fully God, and there is one God."[3] That definition reflects the orthodox position on the Trinity, which has been held from the very early days of church history. There is only one God. But that singular God exists in three distinct persons: the Father, the Son, and the Holy Spirit. The persons of the Trinity always work as one in a spirit of mutual submission which we call love. Each one lives for the sake of the others. It is this triune nature of God that gives sense to the idea that God is eternally love.

We see this mutual, voluntary submission displayed most clearly in the work of God for the salvation of mankind. God loved the world. That is to say that He had a desire to show forth His own character by delivering humans from the hopeless mess they had gotten themselves into. The goal belonged to the Godhead, but in bringing it to pass, each person of the Godhead carried out a different part. God the Father had the plan. He directed the operation. The Son, Jesus Christ, became the sacrifice. He is the person who became flesh so we could know what the true God is really like. Then, on this earth, Jesus accomplished the plan of the Father by the enabling Spirit. We see this clearly in the description of the crucifixion. Jesus, the Son, went through with the sacrifice out of loving submission to His Father. Jesus Christ is the person who would go through that event. Yet, we are told that it was through the eternal Spirit that Jesus offered Himself without spot or blemish (Heb. 9:14). All three persons of the Godhead were present in that sacrifice, loving and supporting one another for a common beneficial end. The Bible can then say that "God was in Christ reconciling the world to Himself" (2 Cor. 5:19).

That is unity in God. Each person of His being constantly flows with a love that is manifested in mutual service. Even though there is a distinction between the Father and the Son, and different roles for each to play to accomplish the will of God, Jesus could still say, "I and the Father are one" (John 10:30).

God brought creation into being to display His greatness. Humanity holds the premiere position in that display. We were made in the image of God. The wording of this event in Genesis 1 is interesting. "God created man [the human race] in His own image, in the image of God He created him; male and female He created them" (Gen. 1:27). It is true that every man and every woman on the earth has the image of God in them. However, if God's directives for mankind to multiply, fill up the earth, and subdue it were to be fulfilled, the male and female dimensions of the human race must work together. Male and female share the image of God, but each is endowed with both capacities and limitations. They necessitate cooperation if they are to experience their full potential and fulfill God's plan. Genesis 2 describes the actual event of the creation of the woman. Eve was formed because there was nothing which "corresponded" to Adam. Eve was not exactly like Adam. She filled out Adam, and Adam filled her out. When the two were joined in mutual love and support, the full potential of each was realized. What is more, in that experience of serving each other, they learned something of the nature of God and placed love on display.

The same is true of God's plan for the church. We are called a "body". We each have gifts and capacities which vary. We have personalities through which we see life differently. We share a common life, the life of Christ in the Spirit, but we are not identical. What is more, no one is complete in himself. The Spirit of God gives gifts to the different members of the body. No one receives enough capacity to fulfill God's purposes on his own. If the will of God is to be done on this earth, we must work together. Loving unity is at the core of this. Listen to what Paul says:

> ...being diligent to preserve the unity of the Spirit in the bond of peace (Eph. 4:3).

> And be subject to one another in the fear of Christ (Eph. 5:21).

> Beyond all these things put on love, which is the perfect bond of unity (Col. 3:14).

When this is so, the same blessing that fell on the Old Testament saints comes to us. "Behold, how good and how pleasant it is for brothers to dwell together in unity! For there the Lord commanded the blessing—life forever" (Ps. 133:1, 3).

With that in mind, we come to this important passage on prayer. Consider the Lord's words: "Again I say to you, that if two of you agree on earth about anything that they may ask, it shall be done for them by My Father who is in heaven. For where two or three have gathered together in My name, I am there in their midst" (Matt. 18:19-20).

In Matthew 18, the Lord has been dealing with several important interpersonal relationships among believers. All point to the importance of the church on the earth, and, more importantly, the high value we should place on other members of the body. He has just spoken on the authority of the church on earth. Now, Jesus turns to the matter of prayer: "Again I say to you" (Matt. 18:19). He assures those who are listening that what He is about to say comes with full authority. That should have been obvious to the disciples, but it is simple for us to forget.

Next, He notes that the promise applies to a gathering as small as two: "If two of you agree" (Matt. 18:19). By itself, we might be tempted to restrict the application of the verse to the apostles. But in verse 20, He simply says that where two or three are gathered (*any* two or three) He would be in the midst. The promise given here extends to the whole church and every member of the church.

The requirement for the two, as they come to pray, is that they agree. Lenski says that the word "agree" means to "agree by talking a thing over."[4] However, we must avoid the conclusion that two believers are free to get together, aim at a target in prayer, and somehow use this promise to force the hand of God. Outside the New Testament, the word for "agree" is most often used of musical instruments which play together. The Greek word means "to sound together". The instruments must be tuned in order to produce music which is pleasant to those who listen. Then, the instruments must agree as to what they are going to play. Either by the direction of a conductor or by following written music, there must be harmony. Musical instruments must agree. That is not to say that they are all the same. The word for "agree" forms the root for the term symphony. A symphony orchestra is made up of many different types of instruments capable of a host of different types of sounds. To make music though, they must "sound together"; they must "agree". Each must adjust to the others and each must, in a sense, submit to the others. Jesus is saying that when even two believers agree in prayer about what needs to happen on this earth, heaven will back them up.

To keep everything in balance, Jesus goes on to tell us how this happens. He expands the scope in Matthew 18:20. Now it is two or three that have come together. They have assembled in Jesus' name. It is not so much that they are coming to the Father counting on Jesus Christ for access to God. While this is true, and we will look more closely at it in the next chapter, here He says that they have met together in Jesus' name. They are there as the representatives of the Lord on this earth. They share a common outlook and are aiming at a common goal. They are not there to fulfill some duty to soothe their consciences. They are not there to coerce the eternal God to bless their lives and plans. They are there to see the purposes of Jesus Christ come to pass, to see the resources of heaven directed to the needs on this earth so that Jesus Christ is glorified. They have come together so that the imperatives we saw in the Lord's Prayer should be fulfilled.

When that takes place, no matter who the persons are, Jesus Christ is in the midst. We need to think a moment about what He is saying. Since God is omnipresent (present equally in every place) the statement is true no matter why people gather together. Jesus is not speaking about that kind of presence. Further, this is something more than the Lord's promised presence to His own disciples. As believers we are united to Jesus Christ. He has become our life. And because He has promised to finish His work in every true believer, we can be assured that He will never leave us or forsake us. But Jesus indicates that there is a dimension of His presence that goes beyond even that. In his commentary on Matthew, William Hendriksen notes that here the idea of God being with us indicates that He is present for the "impartation of strength, direction, protection and consolation."[5] Jesus promises to not only be present but to be actively present, supplying what is necessary so that the goal of the disciples meeting in His name will be fulfilled.

If we take what Jesus says about His presence in verse 20, then return to the teaching on prayer in verse 19, we see the Lord as an active part of the prayer described. His influ-

120

ence, by the Spirit of God, will move people to intercession that will bring the power of heaven to bear in practical ways on earth.

To illustrate what the Lord is saying here, think of the high school experiment with tuning forks. Two forks of the same wavelength are secured in a stand. The first is tapped and begins to sing. If you grab the fork and stop the vibration, the sound continues because the two forks "agreed". The second fork, picking up the vibrations in the air, responds with music. We call it "resonance". It is the reason that a piano is such a rich musical instrument. If you strike the key for middle C on the keyboard, then place your fingers on the corresponding strings to halt the vibration, you will still hear harmonized sound. Every other C in the piano picks up the sound, and every other note in the C chord is affected; chords "sound together".

Before we experienced the new birth, we were dead to God. Nothing about Him resonated in us. When the Spirit brought us to new life in Christ, everything changed. Paul says that "the Spirit Himself testifies with our spirit that we are children of God" (Rom. 8:16). We do not learn that we have God as our Father simply through good teaching. The Spirit resonates in our souls. This resonance is horizontal as well as vertical. In 1 John 3:14, John tells us that we know that we have passed from death to life because we have love for the brothers. When we come to life in the Spirit, we have an immediate affinity with the family of God.

The same is true with the Word of God. Before we knew God, it was a dead book to us. Nothing existed in us that really responded to it. In our new experience, the Bible has an appeal that no other writing can duplicate. It resonates in our hearts. When we speak of it to one another in the body of Christ, it resonates. We are mutually strengthened as we agree together.

What should we learn concerning corporate prayer? First, when believers are unified for the glory of God, their prayers carry a special force before God. This is the necessary balance to what we considered in the first principle concerning prayer: pray to be heard by God, not to impress people around you. At that point, I expressed the idea that private prayer was necessary to develop the habit of God-conscious praying. We need time alone with the Father to keep our outlook pure. That does not imply that there is some inherent problem with group prayer. Once we have learned to pray for the glory of God and not for the approval of others, we are free to enter one of the most powerful dimensions of prayer. I would not hesitate to say that the passage implies that when intercession is offered by two individuals who both live for the purpose of God on this earth, it is more powerful than either of the two alone. We need private prayer, but the potential of our prayer increases as we learn to pray together.

The question should be asked as to why two are better than one in prayer. Jesus does not answer this Himself. I would suggest two related reasons.

Ecclesiastes 4:9 tells us that two are better than one. The reason the Preacher gives for that conclusion is that if one falls, his friend can pick him up. If someone comes to oppose the one, two can put him to flight. The Christian life is a conflict, and most of that conflict is battled out in our minds. The question is whether we will continue to trust God. The value of a committed brother or sister is that the other can hold us up when our hearts are overcome.

I remember a particularly difficult period in my own ministry. I wondered at times if there was any point in continuing. This was not a desire to desert the faith or quit ministry, but simply to move on. I am deeply grateful to the Lord that

He gave me a wife who also loves Him and is determined to live for Him. We both faced a lot of dark days, but never at the same time. Again and again, we picked each other up. As a result, the plan the Father had for us was accomplished.

We face a similar need in prayer. It is interesting that Paul speaks of prayer in Ephesians in connection with spiritual conflict. Part of the reason to put on the spiritual armor is to continue faithfully in prayer. As Americans, we tend to think of warfare in very individualistic terms. We think we need to put on the armor so that we can stand firm as individuals. That of course is true, but in real combat, a soldier does not go into the fight alone. He is not capable of winning alone. The armor is worn so that each Christian can hold his ground in the conflict and support others who are doing the same. Paul urges us to pray for all the saints so that the will of God is done. One of the great values of a regular prayer partner is that they can give mutual encouragement and help.

There is also the purifying aspect of "two together". We would all like to think that if we were wholeheartedly seeking the glory of God, all our prayers would be according to the will of God. But it is not so. We all start with the same set of instructions from God, the Bible. But even if we are committed to follow what we find in the Word of God, we bring bias to our study. Each person brings a distinct personality, a unique set of life experiences, and, sadly, a different collection of weaknesses of the flesh. All these things influence how we read and hear the truth of the Word. Therefore, we are all in an ongoing experience of sanctification. The Spirit of God is working to bring our desire to serve God into reality by systematically eliminating the issues that warp our outlook.

What does that have to do with prayer? The passage in Matthew 18 indicates that the two who have met to pray have come in Jesus' name. They share a desire that the purposes of the Lord be fulfilled. Each brings a whole heart, but it is a whole heart with bias. Yet, because of the love they share for the Lord, Jesus Christ says that He will be present in the meeting. When He is present, He is active. As they pray, He is working in them. "For it is God who is at work in you, both to will and to work for His good pleasure" (Php. 2:13).

John says, "If we ask anything according to His will, He hears us" (1 John 5:14). All true prayer is a request that the Lord will complete the plan He already has. Answered prayer begins with God. How can we know the will of God in each circumstance? We begin by studying the revelation in the Bible. We continue towards an understanding of His will by accepting and submitting to what we find. There is another step which comes in the lives of those who have genuinely entrusted their lives to the Lord in faith. He is actively working to break down our biases, to set us free from our weaknesses, and to make us understand. Paul prays that the Colossian church will be "filled with the knowledge of [God's] will in all spiritual wisdom and understanding" (Col. 1:9). Knowing God's will is much more than discerning whether to take one job or another. Paul is desirous that the church would so deeply understand the Father's plan for the ages that it becomes an almost unconscious controlling influence in their every action. He wants them to think the way God thinks about life.

The Lord also uses other believers to bring this to pass in our lives. When we come together with another believer in His name to pray, He joins our prayer meeting. He works in both parties "to will and to work for His good pleasure" (Php. 2:13), but neither is completely sanctified. Both bring biases, but seldom are the biases the same. As we think and pray about serious issues, we are being worked on by the Lord. In a wonderful way, we work on each other. Iron sharpens iron. Biases cancel each other. Both are brought to a deeper insight into what ought to be done. As we resonate with the Lord and resonate with each other, the purpose of God becomes clearer. Our faith is strengthened, and we become bold to ask.

When we pray in a group, we must make certain that our desire is the honor and glory of the Lord; we must come in Jesus' name. Then we must learn to listen to the prayers of those who have manifested a desire to see the kingdom of God come on the earth. Group prayer has the purifying benefit of making us face and deal with the prejudices we bring to the Lord as we seek His glory. It also strengthens our faith as we have the burden of our hearts confirmed by others, and we symphonize with them before the throne of grace.

CHAPTER TEN

In Jesus' Name

Truly, truly, I say to you, he who believes in Me,
the works that I do, he will do also;
and greater works than these he will do;
because I go to the Father.
Whatever you ask in My name, that will I do,
so that the Father may be glorified in the Son.
If you ask Me anything in My name, I will do it.
John 14:12-14

The final night before the Lord would make His great sacrifice has come. Jesus is alone with the inner circle of His disciples. These men have been the focus of His attention for the last three years. Their training is almost complete. A new juncture has come in the outworking of the great plan of salvation. Jesus will die the next day as a sacrifice for sin. In three days, the Father will declare to the whole world that Jesus is indeed the Son of God by raising Him from the dead. Within six weeks, the Lord will ascend into heaven and assume His place at the right hand of His Father. But that is not the end of the plan. The message of salvation in Jesus Christ must be presented to the whole world. In His final summary message to the disciples, recorded in John 13-17, the Lord outlines the great blessings they will receive in order to carry out that seemingly impossible mission. As the Lord speaks on this subject with his disciples, three changes are enumerated that will supply all they need for the task which will be entrusted to them.

First, the Spirit of God will come upon them in a way

that has never happened. He will be steadily working as they witness to Jesus Christ. He will be a constant companion, ministering both to and through them.

Second, Jesus assures them that, because of what is about to take place, the disciples will share the very life of Christ. Using the picture of a vine and branches, the Lord tells them that they will be united to Him in such a way that they will participate in His life. The Lord and the disciples are to be one. That life of Christ within will lead to both character in their own lives and blessings to those to whom they speak. Their responsibility is to abide, to remain by faith, in that posture.

Finally, the Master tells them that they will have the privilege of praying in His name. Through those prayers, the purposes of the Father will come to pass. Depending on how you read them, the Lord gives either six or seven promises of answered prayer. The collection is stunning.

> Truly, truly, I say to you, he who believes in Me, the works that I do, he will do also; and greater works than these he will do; because I go to the Father. Whatever you ask in My name, that will I do, so that the Father may be glorified in the Son. If you ask Me anything in My name, I will do it (John 14:12-14).

> If you abide in Me, and My words abide in you, ask whatever you wish, and it will be done for you (John 15:7).

> You did not choose Me but I chose you, and appointed you that you would go and bear fruit, and that your fruit would remain, so that whatever you ask of the Father in My name He may give to you (John 15:16).

In that day you will not question Me about anything. Truly, truly, I say to you, if you ask the
Father for anything in My name, He will give it
to you. Until now you have asked for nothing in
My name; ask and you will receive, so that your
joy may be made full (John 16:23-24).

The key which ties all these promises together is the
thought of praying in Jesus' name. But what does that really
mean?

To begin, we must be clear that Jesus was speaking of a
way we pray and not a phrase we use. Earlier in our study,
we saw that there are no magic formulas in prayer. We pray
from our hearts, not simply with our lips. No prayer recorded
in the New Testament contains the phrase "in Jesus' name".
That is important to note. From my earliest days of hearing
people pray, the standard conclusion was, "And this we ask
in Jesus' name. Amen." It was how we knew a person was
finished. It is so ingrained in my mind that I very seldom finish without including these words. As the secular culture began to exclude religion from every area of life, a war erupted
over whether a pastor could use this closing in public. However, a good prayer without this phrase is still accepted by
God, and no bad prayer can somehow be sanctified by the
attachment of the words.

If the phrase is not the point, what does it mean to pray
in Jesus' name? Two great words should help us understand
what is involved in this phrase. Those words are "privilege"
and "responsibility".

First, we have privilege. Every true believer has been
brought into a relationship with Jesus Christ. Paul tells us
(speaking of God), "But by His doing you are in Christ Jesus, who became to us wisdom from God, and righteousness
and sanctification, and redemption" (1 Cor. 1:30). When

we came to Jesus Christ in repentance and faith, we were not only forgiven of sin, but placed in a living union with the Lord. Because of who Jesus is and our identification in Him, we now have a right relationship with God. We considered this in detail in our study of prayer and humility. In one sense, when we say that we pray in Jesus' name, we are saying that the only reason we can come and be heard is because we are associated with Jesus Christ. In Him, we have this great privilege of access to God.

While this is wonderfully true and can be substantiated from various other parts of Scripture, it does not seem to be the primary meaning of what Jesus has to say here. We believe this because of what we read in John 17, as the Lord Himself prays for His church. The Lord is praying here concerning His ministry on earth to the disciples. "While I was with them, I was keeping them in Your name which You have given Me" (John 17:12). The structure "in Your name" is exactly the same as "in My name". Yet here, it cannot have anything to do with a right of access. The Father and the Son had an eternal relationship which was never disrupted by sin. A love existed between them, leading to free and continual fellowship. No mediator was necessary.

What is Jesus referring to when He says He acted in the Father's name? Let's look at the prayer more carefully. "I glorified You on the earth, having accomplished the work which You have given Me to do" (John 17:4). Jesus Christ was sent to earth with a definite purpose. There was a plan to be accomplished. That plan came from the Father. In a sense, since Jesus is the Son, he was sent to do the family business. Jesus lived the most restricted life which has ever been lived. He came at the direction of His Father. He was born into the family that His Father arranged. He started His ministry when the Father determined He was ready. In that ministry, He said that He only did what pleased the Father.

He only spoke the words He was given by the Father. He went to a terrible death on the cross because of the will of His Father. Jesus had no independent life, no other purpose in living than to fulfill the will of His Father. Far from this being a burden to Him, He told His disciples that His food, the thing that gave Him energy and refreshment, was doing the Father's will and seeing blessing come as a result in people's lives (John 4:34).

In the prayer of John 17, the Lord tells us something of what that work entailed. He was given a group of men to work with. He showed them what the Father is like. He gave them instructions from the Father and tirelessly worked to overcome their sin and ignorance. He protected them from danger, both within and without. Those men belonged to His Father and were entrusted to His care. In order to see all that work accomplished, the Lord sanctified Himself. To be "sanctified" means to be set aside for God's purpose and use. What He meant is that He set His life apart for His Father, but that service to God practically meant ministering to particular men. They were men with faces and personalities and weaknesses and spiritual density. They only became the great apostles because Jesus did the family business. That was the Son's responsibility, and as He carried it out, the full authority and power of the Father was at His disposal. Jesus kept the disciples in the Father's name.

Think of what Jesus had been saying to His disciples about the months and years ahead. The Father had a plan for their lives. That plan was not primarily for their comfort or their satisfaction. That plan was to carry out the family business, which we call "the Great Commission". It was not really a volunteer work, but a stewardship entrusted to them. "You did not choose Me but I chose you, and appointed you that you would go and bear fruit" (John 15:16). Jesus reaffirmed the point after the resurrection: "As the Father has sent Me, I also send you" (John 20:21). These men had an enormous responsibility. He sent them out to spread the message of salvation in Jesus Christ. In order to accomplish that work, two provisions were made. First, Jesus would send the Spirit of God to enable His disciples. Second, He granted them the privilege of praying in Jesus' name.

The concept of praying in Jesus' name is simple to understand, though demanding in experience. Many years ago, before credit cards were commonly used, I worked for my dad's construction company. At times, I was commissioned to make the trek to the local lumber yard for materials. In those days, I was given a check. My trips to the lumber yard were in the company's name. They determined what I was to pick up and where to get it. They told me what to do with it after I got it. I used their truck and paid for it with their check. I was not free to use the check for lunch, or to add other materials to the list that I might want for personal projects or for my friends' projects. I could not take the load where I wanted. It had to be delivered where they designated. The arrangement was simple. If I did what they asked me to do, they would pay the bill. The authority was theirs, and the responsibility was also theirs. Working with this illustration, what can we learn about praying in Jesus' name?

First, let's note that praying in Jesus' name defines the *scope* of our prayer potential. When we were born again, we became the children of God. With that great privilege came a real responsibility to glorify God. The Father has a place for each of us to do that; no one is left out. When this life is ended, the only thing that will last is the family business we accomplished. What the Lord said to the disciples that night applies to the whole church. "You did not choose Me but I chose you, and appointed you that you would go and bear fruit, and that your fruit would remain, so that whatever you ask of the Father in My name He may give to you" (John 15:16).

The purpose of our lives is to bless others. He calls that blessing fruit. It is both the loving character of Jesus Christ in us and the life imparting work of the Spirit of God through us. Each of us is surrounded with people in need of the grace of God. As members of the body of Christ, we are each appointed to join the Head in building the church. Each of us has the honor of seeking the Father for this to come to pass. As we saw earlier, the force of vital praying begins with: *Your name has to be honored.* When His glory and His kingdom are at the center of our praying, we are praying in Jesus' name.

The Lord is concerned about our welfare. We have real needs that must be met. However, it is too easy for those needs to become the all-absorbing feature of our praying. As we have said already, praying in Jesus' name is not difficult to understand, but it is demanding in experience. To join the Father in prayer, we must look up to see the needs of those around us and to seek the Father for the application of His salvation to them. This will be costly. Jesus prayed that the disciples would be sanctified in the truth. We tend to restrict the meaning of sanctification to a growth of character. When Jesus sanctified Himself, it meant that He used all the potential of His life, the hours and days he lived on earth, to see to it that the disciples were prepared for what the Father had for them. That absorbed His attention. As He lived that way, despite the sacrifice, He was nourished and invigorated in His own being. In losing His life on earth, He found it.

To pray in Jesus' name is to ask the Father for His plan to come to pass in the real people in our families, churches, workplaces, and neighborhoods. It is to pray that the Father would receive the honor He deserves as people come to Him in repentance and in faith, and then join Him in His great program.

Praying in Jesus' name also defines the *potential* of prayer. When we allow the Spirit of God to bring us to the place where seeking first the kingdom of God becomes our framework for living, the full authority and power of heaven are at our disposal. This alone can explain the free language of the Lord as He speaks about prayer.

> Whatever you ask in My name, that will I do (John 14:13).

> If you ask Me anything in My name, I will do it (John 14:14).

> If you abide in Me, and My words abide in you, ask whatever you wish, and it will be done for you (John 15:7).

These promises are stunning; they are also convicting. The problem of unanswered prayer is real, and a great deal of effort is made to reconcile these verses with our actual prayer experience. People have written whole chapters and even books to address this problem. In His teaching on prayer, Jesus does not. He assumes prayer will be answered. The Lord's teaching on prayer in the upper room echoes all He has taught to that point. The disciples are to pray, seeking first the honor of the Father and the coming of His kingdom. They are to have faith in God and, because of that faith, keep on praying, knowing that everyone who does will receive. They are to encourage one another as they join in prayer, because He is present with them, and is there to give aid. On that difficult night, with confusion and fear swirling in the disciples' minds, Jesus gives them every impression that, even in the hardest circumstances that lie ahead, they will experience the power of God as they live and pray for the

Father's work to be finished in the building of the church. This kingdom focus that results in a display of God's power is what it means to pray in Jesus' name.

Therefore, I would suggest for myself and the rest of the church, if we are not consistently seeing the Lord powerfully intervening in the people and the circumstances around us, we should reflect on whether or not the kingdom of God is actually our priority. Have we responded to the Lord's call? Have we set ourselves apart for selfless service to glorify God through the building of the church of Jesus Christ?

Finally, we should note that praying in Jesus' name guarantees a *result* to our praying. First, there is the result in other people: fruit that remains. There are permanent, life-giving changes in the experience of people around us. Jesus Christ came with the offer of life for anyone who would take it by faith. Some did; most did not. For the ones who did, all the promises of God came to life and blessings began to flow in their experiences. That was because the Lord worked in them. It was also because the Lord prayed for the kingdom of God to come. Consider Jesus' prayer in John 17. He asks for great things. Some remain to be experienced when the plan of God reaches its climax. But much has been realized. Despite the all-out efforts of the world and the devil, the church continues to exist and to prosper. Despite the shortcomings of the people of God, the gospel continues to spread. When we join the Lord in the work of prayer, we are guaranteed that there will be permanent results. Our efforts are never empty in the Lord.

There is a second result. It is fitting that it should be the last thing the Lord says about prayer. "Until now you have asked for nothing in My name; ask and you will receive that your joy may be made full" (John 16:24).

There is no record in the gospels of the disciples praying. They did not accompany the Lord in His prayer vigils. Because the Lord was with them, they could deal directly with Him. They watched Him work, and, in a small way, participated in His ministry. But Jesus says that they had left a whole reserve of possibility completely untapped. Until that time, they had asked for nothing as representatives of Jesus Christ on this earth. It was time for that to change. It was time for them to learn in experience what He had said: "My food is to do the will of Him who sent Me and to accomplish His work" (John 4:34). It was time for them to know the joyous experience of seeing men and women changed and set free by the Father as they prayed.

For others, the result of prayer is spiritual blessing. For the servant who sanctifies himself to do the family business, answered prayer results in joy. A rich and full joy. A joy shared in fellowship with the Father and the Son. A joy that begins here and continues for all eternity.

CITATIONS

1. William Hendriksen, *New Testament Commentary: Exposition of the Gospel According to Matthew* (Grand Rapids: Baker Book House, 1973), 703.

2. Neil Anderson, *The Bondage Breaker* (Eugene: Harvest House Publishers, 1990).

3. Wayne Grudem, *Systematic Theology* (Grand Rapids: Zondervan, 1994), 226.

4. R. C. H. Lenski, *The Interpretation of St. Matthew's Gospel* (Minneapolis: Augsburg Publishing House, 1964), 705.

5. William Hendriksen, *New Testament Commentary: Exposition of the Gospel According to Matthew* (Grand Rapids: Baker Book House, 1973), 705.

ABOUT THE E.I. SCHOOL OF BIBLICAL TRAINING

The E.I. School of Biblical Training was established in 1967 on fifty acres of farmland at the base of Paris Mountain in Greenville, South Carolina. E.I. can be described as an evangelical, non-denominational fellowship holding to fundamental beliefs that define biblical Christianity. Our motto expresses our purpose: Following and Proclaiming Jesus Christ as Lord!

Our two and three year programs aim to bring each student into a vital, enduring fellowship with Jesus Christ through a life of surrender, faith, obedience, prayer, service, and proclamation. We endeavor to create an environment in which an understanding of God's ways is fostered in seeking hearts and a deep love for the Lord is nurtured.

E.I. was established to instill foundational principles. The founder, Joseph S. Carroll, envisioned the need for a Bible school with a new emphasis. His itinerant conference ministry in East Asia convinced him that a Christian life or ministry that does not recognize the primacy of prayer and worship is destined to fail. Over the next years, the Bible school and conference center developed as the Lord not only provided land and buildings but also the fellow workers necessary to begin classes.

Since the first class in 1972, hundreds of students from the United States and internationals from more than 40 countries have found their way to Greenville to see the life of faith lived before them and to begin to walk that path themselves. Many of our graduates are now involved in missions throughout the world. Other graduates pastor churches and are involved in national mission projects, while many more serve the Lord faithfully in local churches.